Narrow Escapes!

BY
MILOSLAV BITTON

MELANDRIUM BOOKS

Published by
MELANDRIUM BOOKS
11 Highway Lane
Keele
Staffs ST5 5AN

© John Bitton

All rights reserved. No part of this publication may be reproduced or transmitted in any other form or by any means, electronic or mechanical including photocopying, recording or any information storage or retrieval system, without prior permission in writing from the publishers.

First published 2013
ISBN 0-9537853-5-1

Designed by **MELANDRIUM BOOKS**
and printed in England by The Book Factory,
Stoke on Trent.

MELANDRIUM BOOKS is proud to publish this book by Miloslav Bitton on behalf of Československá Obec Legionářská v zahraničí (The Association of Czechoslovak Legionaries Abroad).

The book is based on the numerous notes, certificates and documents collected over the years by the author and compiled into a chronological narrative at the beginning of the new millennium. Covering the years 1919 to 1949, it tells the story of his childhood in the Ukraine and Czechoslovakia, of the outbreak of World War II and his experiences running a clandestine escape route, and his service in the army in the Middle East and the Royal Air Force in Britain.

In September 1945 he returned to Prague with his English wife to pursue a career in the Czechoslovak Air Force. After the communist coup in 1948, they were forced to flee the country and again start a new life, this time in England.

This book is sold in aid of
Československá Obec Legionářská v zahraničí.

Dedication

This book is dedicated to my family, friends and comrades in arms.

Nadporučík, First Lieutenant Miloslav Kratochvíl, 1946

Contents

Chapter 1	**The Ukraine**	1
1919 1926	Alexandrovka	
Chapter 2	**Czechoslovakia I**	7
1926 1927	Alžbětín Dvor	
1927	Hviezdoslavov	
1929	Némétsók	
1930	Štvrtok Na Ostrove	
1931 33	Nagy Hegy	
1933 39	Bratislava	
Chapter 3	**Czechoslovakia II**	32
1939	September December	
1940	January May	
Chapter 4	**Middle East**	49
1940	June December	
1941	January December	
1942	January December	
Chapter 5	**England I**	82
1943	January July	
Chapter 6	**Canada**	95
1943	August December	
1944	January April	
Chapter 7	**England II**	110
1944	April December	
1945	January December	
Chapter 8	**Czechoslovakia III**	134
1945	September December	
1946	January December	
1947	January December	
1948	January May	
Chapter 9	**England III**	170
1948	June December	
1949	January October	
Postscript		
Appendix	Military Service	
	Decorations, medals and badges	

Chapter 1: The Ukraine

1919 – 1926 Alexandrovka

My very first memory, and one I will always carry with me, is the blaze of a huge stack of straw set on fire in our back yard and all the people rushing to extinguish it. For obvious reasons, this is also the most vivid recollection I have of my earliest years in Alexandrovka[1], Ukraine, where I was born on 14th October 1919. After a few hours, when the fire had been brought under control and the grown-ups had discussed how it could have started, their attention was turned to the three or four children, myself included, who had been seen playing with matches near the stack. The search for the culprits soon began and all were accounted for, except me. The search was intensified, all the outhouses and hideaways in our yards and, of course, the house, were checked. They shouted out my name, imploring me to come out and promising that nothing would happen to me. I was terrified and didn't dare come out of my hiding place.

Eventually I was discovered hiding in one of the bedrooms, tucked away under a bed. After a lot of pleading I admitted taking the matches from the kitchen, and setting light to a small heap of straw in a tunnel under the stack, so that we could sit round the flames and keep warm. Within seconds the fire had spread everywhere inside the tunnel and we just managed to escape, each one of us heading for somewhere to hide.

Living on a farm, this loss was a great setback as we wouldn't have any more straw until the harvest some months later – my parents explained this to me some time later. Straw was used both for fodder for the livestock and for fuel for heating the house. Straw and dung were mixed together and formed into briquettes, we called them *kirpič,* which were then left to dry in the open air.

All our neighbours were farmers. You could see horses, cattle, carts and farm machinery everywhere – the village bustled with activity. We occasionally took our produce by cart to the market in Birzula[2], the nearest town about 25 km away. I used to look forward to these trips and was always rewarded with sweets. My job was to make sure that no one made holes in the sacks of grain that we had brought

---

[1] Now Oleksandrivka
[2] Now Kotovsk

to sell – unless my father gave a potential buyer permission to do so. The buyer would then use a special sampler to determine the quality of the goods. When a serious offer for the purchase of the goods or livestock had been made it would be followed by rounds of hand slapping until a final price had been agreed on, after which the two parties invariably disappeared for a drink, usually vodka.

I only have a limited recollection of the different market stalls but I do remember the sweet stalls and the stalls selling dried fish, which were hung on a line, and sometimes salted fish. Travelling to the market was not always easy as the weather often made the roads, which were not surfaced, impossible for a horse and cart. My father would even try to get there with our two-wheeled cart but he often had to turn back because of the mud. If there was an urgent errand, he would ride to the town on horseback.

Our back garden was full of fruit trees and I was just as good at climbing them as I was at walking. I fell out of the trees quite a few times but this did not put me off climbing some really high ones. At least I didn't suffer from vertigo.

Tomatoes, cucumbers, honeydew melons and water melons grew in abundance. Whole watermelons were stored in barrels, where they were preserved until the next spring by packing them between layers of sand and salt. We also made our own sauerkraut and my contribution to making it perfect was to tread it down into the storage barrel with my bare feet. However, before I was allowed to do this, I had to spend some time soaking in our bathtub which, in fact, was just an ordinary barrel! And everyone baked their own bread; there were no shops of any kind in the village.

I had many friends and we used to play hide-and-seek or just wander around in the village. Sometimes we ventured to the woods a few kilometres away to pick wild strawberries or bring back acorns. On one of these expeditions we found some large bones and brought them home. Instead of being told off we were praised for our good deed and rewarded with sweets. Later a large group of grown-ups went off to bring back the rest of the bones – they were going to be used for making soap.

I also remember when three or four men in uniform, and carrying guns, came to see my father one spring. One of them stood at the front door. I was allowed to stand close to my father; I just couldn't keep my eyes off their revolvers. Somehow, I seemed to have embarrassed my father, the men were teasing me and I was giving them all the wrong answers. Much later on, my father explained the consequences of their visit: as he was the village elder, they had come to inform him about how much grain all the families would have to deliver to the state. However, the grain that we had saved had already been sown for that year's crop; there was nothing left. Despite offering cattle or even money to the 'authorities' to meet their demands, he was put in jail until other villagers could sell off some cattle and buy grain with the money! He was incarcerated for about a month, as none of the nearby villages had any grain to spare and it had to be bought some distance away.

Across the road from our house was the village school and it was used for a number of different purposes. During the day, there were lessons for the children and, in the evenings, the village elders would meet here. I especially remember one gathering at the school with both parents and children present when a few of the teenagers were publicly punished for their misbehaviour. They had to bend over and receive a few strokes of a twisted rope. Being the youngest in the family, with three brothers and three sisters, I was a bit of a mummy's boy and was protected from this sort of strict punishment, but I do remember my brothers and sisters getting a taste of it.

I started school when I was five, attending a class for a few hours every day. We were taught Czech although this was most probably not allowed. Once, when some Russians came to visit us, all our copybooks had to be hidden and books in Russian were produced and we had to pretend that it was a normal subject. I can also still see myself standing next to the blackboard, adding up columns of figures, competing at the same time with a girl of my own age doing the same sums.

My greatest joy, however, was to get home and play with my friends and my favourite pet, a lamb. We had become inseparable and it would follow me absolutely everywhere. Problems arose when I started school, as it would come along too and someone would have to bring it back. Eventually, it had to be locked up.

At harvest time there was great activity on the farm. The crops were gathered in from the fields – some sort of machine was used to cut and bind the stalks of grain after which they were brought home to be heaped ready for threshing. There were long pipes attached to the thresher for removing the chaff. The yield was graded and stacked in sacks in different piles. Straw, a very important commodity on the farm, was also neatly stacked, everyone hoping that it would last until the next harvest. Lots of men from the surrounding Russian villages used to come looking for farm work and they were taken on as required.

As far as I can remember, my mother only cooked two different dishes: *mămăligă*, which was made from ground corn and prepared like porridge and served with milk, and *borscht* – traditional beetroot soup, thick with vegetables and sometimes even with some meat added. I suppose there must have been some other dishes too!

One day there was a gathering in the village hall and everyone became very excited. At home my mother kept telling me that I was soon going to meet my brother Jaroslav, after we had moved to a new home in a new country. Until then I was not aware that I had another brother. After some deliberation and a few more meetings with the village elders, my parents decided to proceed with their application to travel to a new home in Czechoslovakia. We all had to go to Birzula to have our photographs taken. We also went to visit someone in Odessa. For the first time in my life I saw the sea and really big boats. A rowing boat took us to a nearby island – the boat was so full that the water nearly came over the sides – and I was terrified of drowning. My father held my hands in a firm grip and this saved the situation. I was assured that nothing could happen and, to prepare me for the return trip, I was told I could have any sweets I wanted. That really calmed me down!

Quite soon after our visit to Odessa a lot of people came to see us. We also had a photograph taken in front of the house shortly before our departure. And then the day came and we started off on our journey to the station. A large procession of relatives and friends accompanied us. After lots of hugs and kisses we were left alone in the waiting room.

As a special treat my parents had bought me a clockwork car, you just wound it up and it would go on for ever. I played with it until the train came. Travelling on a train with large carriages and sleeping accommodation was quite an exciting experience. Six people could sleep in each compartment, which had shelves that could be used as bunks. The guard came round in the evening and locked each compartment for safety.

When we reached the Polish borders we had to change trains as they ran on different gauges. There was also quite a lengthy delay because of the strict Russian customs procedures. Our bundles of luggage, our samovar and some suitcases were taken to the customs hall where uniformed and armed officials called my father to identify his possessions. I insisted on going with him and they gave their permission. The search began with our bundles of bedding and our *peřiny,* large feather-filled duvets. They poked their hands into them, feeling for anything hidden inside. Then they looked through the suitcases. Nothing was found in our luggage that would contravene the regulations. The next thing I saw was them asking for my father's cap and jacket. The cap had a hard black peak and this was neatly cut with a knife and prised apart – this was all part of their search for contraband. The shoulders and sleeves of his jacket were treated in the same way. After signing some documents we were able to join the rest of our family in the waiting room. When my mother saw us coming she looked very afraid and was crying. We had been away rather a long time and the state of my father's clothing did not improve matters. However, she was soon busy with a needle and thread, repairing the damage. Our journey then continued through Poland; we were on our way to our new homeland – Czechoslovakia.

Our family house in Alexandrovka, the Ukraine, 1926. Built by my parents Pavel and Marie Kratochvíl.

Family photograph taken in 1923/24. Left to right; Ludvík, Božena, Pavel, Emilie, myself, Marie and Růžena. Jaroslav had already left for Czechoslovakia.

Chapter 2: Czechoslovakia I

1926 – 1927 Alžbětín Dvor

We arrived in Czechoslovakia in July 1926, disembarking at a very small station in Alžbětín Dvor, just 15 km south-east of Bratislava. A few people had come to meet us, our luggage was loaded onto a cart and we all walked the short distance to my parents' friend's house where we stayed for a few days. Their family name was Hulka. Then we moved to another house in the centre of the village and we had all the rooms to ourselves. The house belonged to some Volynians, people who came from Volyn in Poland. I soon found many new friends, learned new games and had a great time exploring the new surroundings.

In early September, I started going to school at Miloslavov, a village about 3 km away, as there was no local school. There was quite a gang of us, always hurrying to get there on time. Coming home invariably took much longer, as I always got involved in a game or a fight! I soon started to blend in with the other children and managed to apply myself to my schoolwork. We also started attending a Baptist chapel on Sunday morning and in the afternoon we went to Sunday school.

After making some enquiries and writing to various people, my father managed to locate my brother Jaroslav and set out to bring him home. There was a magnificent reunion party and I had suddenly gained another brother, someone I couldn't really remember but had only heard about. For days, we listened to his tales and heard about all the kind people who had looked after him whilst we were still in Russia. Although he was three years older than I was, he was only slightly taller. We became very close in no time and I could always rely on his support if there was any trouble with my friends.

1927 Hviezdoslavov

Our next move, in 1927, was to Hviezdoslavov, close to Kvetoslavov, a village about 4 km away. Preparing for this move took quite a long time because the house we were moving to, in the centre of the village, first had to be fumigated. As I accompanied my father almost everywhere, I could see how this was done. To begin with, all the windows were properly closed and sealed off with rags and paper. Then my father made some sort of contraption in the middle of one of the rooms and started a really good blaze in it, mainly feeding the fire with leather, mostly old shoes and boots. When the rooms had become full of smoke he left the fire smouldering and we left, closing and sealing the door behind us. We put a notice on the front door, 'Fumigation in Progress'. Someone was engaged to check on the house now and again and after about a week we came back. My father was satisfied with the results and the next step was to thoroughly ventilate the whole house. As soon as it was possible to go indoors, we all joined in to scrub it from top to bottom and then redecorate it. The move was easy to undertake, having only beds and bedding and a few pieces of furniture.

My new school was just around the corner, housed in a large hall, where all the children, irrespective of age, sat together. Our teacher was Mr. Olinhart. Discipline was enforced very strictly and promptly – a few strokes on our hands or buttocks for minor faults and, for serious misbehaviour, kneeling in the corner on dried peas. It was no use complaining to my parents; they would always say, "You must have deserved it", and would sometimes punish me again themselves.

Everyone in Hviezdoslavov was involved in agriculture. Roads were made with fairly large ditches on either side, always full of water after a rainfall. Nothing was mechanised and we had to use horses for everything. When our cows were let out to graze they had to be kept on leads as the only pasture available was the grass on the sides of the roads. Horse-drawn carriages provided the only means of transport in the village. The railway station on the Bratislava - Komarno line was about 1 km away and there was also a line to Šamorín, a town with a population of about ten thousand, mostly Hungarians. On the very rare occasions when cars came through our village, all the children would run into the clouds of dust, playing a sort of hiding game. My mother would not be pleased at all and used to put me in a tub to wash all the dust off. In fact, almost every day, after playing with my friends, I had to be given a good scrub in our bathtub. There was no street lighting in the village and very few of the buildings had electricity. Our house was lit by paraffin lamps.

I still remember a few of the names of my classmates, perhaps the ones I used to play with the most: Jaroslav Račinský and his brother Dobroslav, Vašek Tuček, Dobroslav Provazník, Antonin Večeřa, Vlasta and Máňa Malá, Sečanský, Petrák, Brodky, Roman, Svoboda and Vidor (his mother owned the only pub in the village). Our favourite game was football and, as we always played and ran about bare-footed, we played football bare-footed too. We boys also enjoyed playing a game which we called *tipcat*. You had to hit a wooden stick, about an inch thick and five inches long and tapered at both ends, so that it jumped into the air and then hit it again, trying to hit it the furthest. Sometimes we used to roam through nearby fields, hoping to catch a hare or a partridge with our sticks! Our favourite, but forbidden, playing ground was the local gravel pit. It covered an enormous area and was perfect for hide-and-seek, but it was dangerous as there were some very deep water holes. We kept our adventures there a secret, never letting on at home.

Suddenly, one day in 1929, there was talk in the village that the Račinskýs were going to emigrate to Canada and that meant I was going to lose my best friend Jaroslav. We had a school photograph taken at their request – hoping that they would then remember us in far-away Canada. There was a farewell party and I remember enjoying myself very much, not realising that I might never see my friend again.

Without us knowing, my father had started to learn to ride a bicycle. He had managed to borrow one and used to take it just outside the village to practise. When I found out about this I would stealthily creep up on him and observe his rather painful experiences – he used to come home with bruises or with tears in his jacket and trousers. However, he would never let anyone steady him or help in any way.

Sometimes he caught me spying on him and I was told not to tell anyone about him falling off. Eventually, he accepted help from someone from outside the village and he soon picked up the art of cycling. Shortly after this, a new bicycle, a 'Star', appeared in our house. It had detachable handlebars and these were always hidden when it was not in use, effectively preventing anyone else from learning how to ride it. My brothers and sisters waited anxiously for permission to do so. There were very few bicycles about and most journeys had to be made either on horseback or by train. After a lot of pressure from the whole family, my father allowed my eldest brother to have a try and, to my father's great astonishment, he managed to learn how to cycle in just one day! Secretly, Ludvík gave us all lessons. Being the youngest and small, I had to cycle with one of my legs through the frame, under the crossbar. Father eventually realised that the cycle was in constant use and not to be found when he needed it. So he started locking up the handlebars again. By now, however, my brother Ludvík could even ride it without the handlebars! Father often said that he wished he had bought a horse instead; at least it would always have been at hand when needed! The price of a bicycle then was about 1,000 crowns – a good horse would have cost about the same.

This was the year when our new village school was completed and furnished. There was a lot of talk and excitement. We were divided into different classrooms and other children from the neighbourhood also started to attend, among them quite a few Hungarians. We all had to bring a spare pair of shoes and put them on before entering our classrooms. However, this rule was eventually abandoned, as there were too many problems with spare shoes lying everywhere.

The school was centrally heated and in each classroom, high up on the walls, we also had electric radiator panels. Just before the summer vacations a school trip to Brno was organized. We were all very excited, especially about the long train ride. The whole trip cost 12 crowns, everything included. In Brno, we were accommodated in a school where meals were also provided. We paid visits to the underground caves in Macocha and the ancient castle and prison in Špilberk, the main reasons for our three-day trip.

1929 Némétsók

Again, quite suddenly, there was talk at home about moving, this time to Némétsók[3], a small Hungarian settlement about 1 km away. Apparently we had been waiting for the piece of land which had been previously allocated to my father by the Czechoslovak authorities. This land had been part of a very large estate belonging to Count Esterházy and had been taken over by the authorities to be divided among the new settlers in the area. We duly moved into a temporary two-bedroom dwelling in a row of terraced farm workers' cottages in Némétsók, in a predominantly Hungarian area (they used to work for the Count on the estate).

I soon found many new friends and playing with them all the time I learnt to speak Hungarian, which was a great help to my parents in their new surroundings. My sisters – Emilie, Růžena and Božena –

---

[3] Now Podhaj

found it difficult to adapt, the language barrier being the main obstacle. And some of the Hungarians were not at all pleased about our arrival.

In the meantime, our new house was nearing completion, only about 300 m away. It stood on its own land, fenced in all around, and included large stables, a cowshed and a piggery that had all previously been used by the estate. Gradually, we acquired some horses and other farm livestock and moved into our new house. It was very large indeed. There were four bedrooms, a lounge, a kitchen, a pantry and two adjoining rooms for handling the milk and farm produce. The large concreted area in the piggery, with pools for the pigs to wallow in, became my favourite place for playing and riding my scooter, a Christmas present from Růžena. My Hungarian playmates now came only if they were invited. Quite a few of them used to go to the new school in Hviezdoslavov and out of school we always spoke Hungarian among ourselves. My sisters and brothers had many friends in Hviezdoslavov and used to go there quite often. They also participated keenly in all the social activities. Ludvík played the trumpet in the brass band and was also keen on football and volleyball and other sports. My sisters were active in the local theatrical society and also took part in the Beseda national country dancing group.

1930 Štvrtok Na Ostrove

My father was not very happy with the land that had been allocated to him in Németsók. It had very large areas full of gravel and consequently our crop yield was very poor. Not being able to acquire or rent more land for farming, he decided to sell up. This meant that we would have to move again and Štvrtok Na Ostrove, about 2 km away and with its mostly Hungarian population, became our new home.

At the end of June, before moving, I went to Šamorín to sit the secondary school entrance exams. (At about this time, Jaroslav had already left for Bratislava and had become an apprentice in a grocery shop.) I was successful and in September my problems started! First, I had to walk about 3 km to the station and then travel about 25 minutes by train. However, about three months later, after moving to Štvrtok Na Ostrave, there was no other way to get to the station, now about 5 km away, than by bicycle. And, shortly afterwards, when the winter had set in, this became impossible. My father took me to the station a few times by horse-drawn sledge but this was not a long-term solution. In the end, it was decided that I would have to find lodgings in Šamorín. With the help of my school friends I found somewhere to stay. It was with a Hungarian family and not very far away from the school.

I was very comfortable there and well looked after, and my reasonable knowledge of their language helped too. The father was an elderly man, retired and in very poor health. He used to be a well-known local mason. He was a regular churchgoer, a Roman Catholic, and I used to go to mass with him on Sundays, just to keep him company, as he would say! In my spare time, we used to play cards together.

Šamorín was the main town in our district with quite a few shops, banks and government offices as well as a hospital and military barracks. The large open market was well stocked with produce and livestock from the surrounding farms. In the spring, I came home and recommenced my long journeys to the train. Most of the time I was able to use the family bicycle and sometimes I was able to stay with friends in Hviezdoslavov overnight.

1931 – 33 Nagy Hegy
In the summer of 1931 we found ourselves on the move again. My father had managed to rent a farm some 12 km to the southeast and with the help of our friends and two or three journeys by wagon, we managed to move our belongings and settle in Nagy Hegy. The farm was quite isolated, on the edge of a fairly large wood. Our nearest neighbouring villages were Bellova Ves, about 1½ km away, and Blahová, about 3½ km away, both recently built settlements. The people who lived here were mostly from Moravia, some were from Bohemia, and had come to farm the land acquired by the State from Count Esterházy.

To continue my secondary education I had to go to Dunajská Streda, a town approximately halfway between Bratislava and Komárno. To get to the railway station, I had to walk or cycle about 6 km. The road went through a Hungarian village called Nagy-Lég[4] from where it was another 2 km to the Veľký Lég station. Soon after 7 o'clock in the morning I boarded the train and reached Dunajská

---
[4] Now Velky Leg

Streda at about 8.20. Those of us who had come by train were allowed to go straight to our classes where lessons started at 9. My daily routine entailed getting up at 5 and leaving home by 5.30 to catch the train at 7.05. In the afternoons, I got home by about 5.30. I was only able to use our bicycle on very rare occasions, as we were so isolated and it was always needed at home.

The roads were very bad, often just tracks with ditches on either side. When it rained even the horses pulling the wagons would sink deeply into the mud and progress was very slow. In the winter, I was sometimes taken to Nagy-Lég by sledge and on extremely bad days on horseback. The last 2 km before the station the road had a better surface, now and then being repaired with gravel. This was, perhaps, because Nagy-Lég had a post office, a *četník*[5] station and a Bat'a shoe shop. Along the route to the station was a large forest where there was a very large country house belonging to a Hungarian Count.

Travelling through Nagy-Lég village used to scare me because, now and then, some of the boys used to chase me and even throw stones at me. The *četníks* were informed and I was gradually able to pass without being attacked. Eventually, they became quite friendly, perhaps because my brother Ludvík had started to play football for their local team where he even became a bit of a celebrity.

The land we were now renting comprised two large areas and my father was very satisfied. There were no hedges anywhere between the fields and just a single furrow, with a stone to mark each end, separated our land from that of our neighbours.

During my summer holidays, I was fully involved in work around the farm. We now had 5 or 6 horses, 8 cows, about 12 to 15 pigs, 350 chickens, 20 geese, 30 ducks and 30 to 40 turkeys. The wood, just at the back of our house, was a great asset, not only for the poultry but for supplying us with fuel too. The house we lived in was fairly large with three bedrooms, a hall, a kitchen and a dining room. Adjoining there were stables for the horses and sheds for the cows. There was also a large shed for poultry and the piggery was about 50 m away from the house. Immediately behind was a very large shed for all of our farm equipment. About 30 m from our house lived a Hungarian labourer and his large family; there were eight children up to the age of 14. He worked on our farm as a casual labourer but this was not

---

[5] Police or gendarme

sufficient to keep his family. His house, the only building apart from ours, had a hall and one room, which served as their kitchen, dining room and bedroom. There were two beds, a table, and some benches and the floor was made of hard uneven trodden-in soil, with no covering whatsoever. We were able to pass on many useful things including some furniture. Their existence, however, must have been very difficult indeed.

There was no running water in our house, but there was a well about 30 m from the front door. Our dairy products, butter and cottage cheese, were kept in the well and once a week one of my sisters would take the produce to the market – on our bicycle. In winter and in bad weather, a horse and cart had to be used to do the job. We very rarely bought any meat, I only remember us buying beef, which we used to boil. We used to kill our own pigs, which provided us with pork fat and meat. The meat was always cooked and put in large jars. These were then sealed with hot pork fat.

Slaughtering a pig used to be a great and exciting occasion, especially for me. I had to hold a bowl to collect the blood, which was later used for black puddings. Then we covered the pig with straw and set it alight to burn off the bristles. In order to do this properly, the pig had to be turned over and the process repeated. It was then placed on a large wooden board and scrubbed well with hot water. A butcher would then cut up the pig into joints and the rest was up to us. There was always plenty to do; the fat was rendered down, and black and white puddings and brawn were made. Chickens were always readily available and it used to be my job to catch and deal with them. Ducks, geese and turkeys were always raised for the market, mostly for the Christmas table.

During our first year on the farm I decided to start breeding rabbits and the venture was so successful that I was even able to sell some rabbit meat to my parents! After only two years, I was able to sell my rabbits to families in the nearby villages and it became quite a thriving business. At its peak, I had about 350 rabbits to look after, with some help, of course, from my brother Ludvík.

I soon made friends with boys from the neighbouring villages, especially from Bellova Ves; I remember Koplík and Musil. In the summer, our wood was the great attraction – we used to go hunting with sticks for wild rabbits, hares, partridges and magpies. We rarely had any luck but we always had a good time. Occasionally, the whole school came to our farm for an outing and we used to organise games for everyone. In my spare time, though mainly on Sundays, I used to go to Bellova Ves to see my friends and play volleyball and football. In the summer, we were always barefooted and all the games were played without shoes. In the week, during my summer vacation, I was now old enough to help with the ploughing and gathering in maize and turnips. We had a very large vegetable garden, with white and red cabbage – we used to make our own sauerkraut – peas, beans, tomatoes, watermelons, honeydew melons, strawberries and raspberries. We also had lots of fruit trees, with plums, cherries, apples, pears, walnuts and apricots. We didn't have a greenhouse. One year, my father decided to plant sunflower seeds so that we could make sunflower oil. A long strip of land, about four acres, was duly planted and everything was very promising until the harvest. The ripe seeds attracted huge colonies of birds and this created a really big problem – how were we going to save at least some of our harvest? For quite a few days, it was my job to walk along the strip of sunflowers and shoot in the air, just to scare off the birds. This effort was only partially successful. Our experiment with sunflowers was never repeated.

During our second year on the farm, my father and Ludvík, who had taken a course in agriculture, decided to put into practice some of his newly gained skills. We acquired some old farm machinery, a Massey Harris harvester, for cutting and binding our crop. The machinery had not been used for a few years as it had been left behind on one of the large estates that had been expropriated by the government from its Hungarian landowners. After carrying out some repairs, we were able to put it to use. The machine was pulled by four horses and I used to sit on the leading horse to guide it. Lots of locals, especially Hungarians, came to admire this new method of harvesting.

At that time, farmers in the neighbouring Czech villages were using farm equipment that was not quite up to our standard – their machines could cut the crop but couldn't tie it into bundles, which meant that this had to be done by hand. When the whole crop had been gathered together in our yard, arrangements were made to thresh it and this usually took 3 to 4 days. Everything was then weighed and 8½ percent of the yield was given in payment for the use of the threshing equipment and the people who manned it. Most of the grain was immediately taken to a communal barn for storage. The remainder was stored in our attic for sowing the following year and for making flour. We used to take five or six bags of wheat to a mill and wait for our turn to have it ground. This was done to our requirements and all the by-products were also saved, to be used for fodder. A percentage was kept for the mill's services; otherwise they had to be paid for in cash. Our nearest mill was about 30 km away but we only had to go there three or four times a year; there was always a good stock of flour in the attic.

Mother baked bread once a week. The dough was prepared one day in advance and when the bread oven was lit it was placed on a warm spot close by to rise. Eight or nine loaves were baked, each individually shaped in round straw baskets. Each loaf weighed about 2 kg. As I was the baby in the family, there was always one small loaf baked especially for me! Freshly baked bread spread with pork fat and sprinkled with sugar was the best treat I knew. There were always *koláče*, small cakes, in the house, some of them specifically baked to keep for special occasions or when visitors called. My sisters, who were quite a bit older than I was, now had boyfriends and they used to call by on Sundays. Sometimes there would be parties too.

During the winter, activities on the farm slowed down considerably, although the cows and horses still had to be fed and the horses also had to be exercised. The first snow usually fell around Christmas time and stayed until early spring. The temperature used to drop to –10 °C or even –20 °C. However, there were always lots of crisp and sunny days.

My journey to school was never affected by the weather; I used to be warmly dressed and with my high boots I was able to get through even the worst of the winter blizzards. During the whole school year, two terms, I was only absent on two occasions due to some sort of illness. And I was very pleased that we did not have to attend classes on Saturdays. This was because there was a very large Jewish community in Dunajská Streda, the children making up almost a third of the pupils. During the winter I had to do my homework as soon as I got home; there was no electricity, only paraffin lamps. However, all the rooms in the house were warm. There was a high tiled wood-burning stove built between the two bedroom walls. Coal was very expensive, though readily available from a coal merchant some 20 km away.

In the winter, my sisters used to organize evening hen plucking sessions, usually meeting four or five times, with a party to celebrate at the end. A dozen or so girls and some of their boyfriends would pluck feathers for their *peřiny* and cushions for the girls' bottom drawers.

To supplement our meals, especially in winter, we used to shoot rabbits in our wood. At one corner of our yard there was a special dugout, well camouflaged but terribly cold, and from there we could occasionally shoot a hare. Sometimes, in the height of a blizzard and under the pretext of having to exercise the horses, Ludvík would take a sledge over the fields to see if he could catch some partridges. He invariably came home with about eight or so. I used to accompany him and we had to be pretty smart, as the *četníks* would have investigated if they had heard shots being fired in the open.

Being very isolated, we had permits to keep guns and kept two rifles for hunting as well as a revolver. Cartridges were expensive and we used to make our own. There were frequent robberies in other villages and my father was always on the alert. Our five dogs always gave us ample warning when anyone approached our farm. On quite a few occasions my father and Ludvík went out armed to investigate a possible intruder. After firing a few shots in the air, everything usually calmed down and I could go to sleep again. On one occasion, at about three in the morning, there was quite a commotion in the house. Someone had startled my sisters in their bedroom by repeatedly knocking and scratching on their windows.

Father quietly opened one of the back windows and Ludvík went up and opened the attic window. On a given signal, they both opened fire and after about 10 minutes all was quiet again, even the dogs stopped barking. A few days later, the *četníks* called, offering their apologies – they had only wanted to frighten my sisters! And they thought that our shooting was pretty accurate.

By this time, I was now thirteen, I was also allowed to take one of the guns and go into the wood to shoot crows and magpies. The birds used to steal our chickens when they were left unguarded. My favourite dog, Brok (Pellet), who was half Alsatian, was always by my side. He used to accompany me for at least a mile on my way to the train every day – and wait for my return in the afternoon. On my command, he would catch chickens for me, destined for the table, but he would never actually harm them. There was a perfect understanding between us. The other four dogs were good guard dogs and were chained to long wires at various points in the yard. There were also three or four cats but neither the cats nor the dogs were allowed inside the house, though on very rare occasions Brok would be exempted from this strict rule.

1933

In the spring of my final year at secondary school, we were asked what we would like to do next. My ambition was to sit the entrance exams for the Commercial Academy, a four-year course, or at least qualify for a two-year course at a business school. However, this would have created a number of problems and great expense for accommodation, as I would have to live so far away from home – the nearest school was in Bratislava – and this was simply not within my parents' means. After numerous discussions about my future, it was finally decided that I should learn the butcher's trade. However, this idea was eventually dropped when it was realised that the heavy sides of beef or pork, which you had to carry on your shoulders, would be too much for me, as I was rather tall and thin! Finally it was decided that I was to follow in Jaroslav's footsteps and learn all about the grocery trade.

1933 – 39 Bratislava

After my last long summer vacation in 1933 I started my apprenticeship in a small grocery shop in Bratislava. Mr Horak, the proprietor, came to an agreement with my father whereby I would work without wages during my apprenticeship and my father would make a contribution to my costs, as I would be living in.

The working conditions were very hard indeed. I had to get up at 5 a.m. and start the day by delivering milk to quite a large area. The shop was just on the outskirts of Bratislava, beyond and above the main railway station on a hillside. Our customers were scattered along the valley and hillsides. Usually there was an order in the milk bottle for the commodities required and even the smallest order, no matter how far away, had to be attended to.

The shop stocked everything, including coal and paraffin. In the winter I managed to deliver the heavy sacks of coal or potatoes on a sledge, otherwise I had to use a cart and, to reach some of the remote houses up on the hillsides, I had to carry the loads on my back. Almost every morning, I was sent to the open market in Bratislava, about 3 km away, to get vegetables and other wares for the business. I was able to use a bicycle to get there but on the return journey I had to push the bike, carrying the load over the crossbar, as it was mostly uphill.

I found my work very hard indeed and being away from home did not help either. I was terribly homesick. However, I was determined to carry on, especially knowing that my brother Jaroslav had gone through similar ordeals during his training. At Christmas I went home for a two-day visit. My parents raised an awful lot of questions about my well-being as I had become even thinner. I did not complain, hoping that my apprenticeship would shortly take a turn for the better. Unfortunately I was wrong, and only on rare occasions was I allowed to serve a customer in the shop. The owner, Mr. Horak, or his wife, both in their mid-fifties, did this themselves, making me and the maid perform all the menial jobs.

Jaroslav was now a fully-fledged assistant and was able to call on me now and again, usually on a Sunday. I was not allowed to go out at all during the week and only with Mr. Horak's consent on Sundays. After hearing me out, Jaroslav suggested I should tell our parents about the conditions I had to endure. This happened sometime in the spring when my father came to visit and saw that I was in a rather poor state. It was decided that enough was enough and an arrangement was made between my father and Mr. Horak for me to work until the end of my notice and then to come home.

1934

With Jaroslav's help, my father approached the Bratislava Chamber of Trade and put my name down on a waiting list for apprenticeship openings. Within days I was notified about a vacancy and I accompanied my father to introduce myself and hear about the conditions. Everything appeared to be acceptable and I was eager to commence work again. On 7th May I started my apprenticeship at *Jan Matys Colonial*, in the Vajnorská district of Bratislava. I lived in with my employer, whose semi-detached house at 5 Sliezska Ulice was only about five minutes away from the shop.

Being the only employee, I was immediately taught how to handle goods and customers and within a short time I had become quite useful and was well-liked by our customers. Again, my day started early. I had to get up at 5 and by 5.30 we were in the shop, preparing milk and bread rolls for my rounds. I had a special basket that I could strap on my back for deliveries, and when I had to deliver to customers living on the edge of our area I used a bicycle.

Most of our customers were civil servants who lived in a huge five-storey block of flats, with twelve staircases. Our shop and a chemist's, next door, were the only businesses in the block. We closed for lunch between 1.30 and 2.30 and closed for the day at 6. During the summer I had to do the morning milk round on Sundays between 7 and 9.30. After work I was not allowed to go out, there was always something to be done – cleaning shoes, polishing the floor or looking after their young daughter Lída, always known as Liduška.

On Sunday mornings we all went to church for the eleven o'clock service. The church was the *Českobratrská Jednota Hussite*, the Hussite Czech Brethren Unity Church in Cukrová Ulice, about 3 km away towards the centre of Bratislava. We always went by tram and after the service we came straight home for lunch. We would also go to the six o'clock service, getting home again by 8.

My work was never very easy, but it was so much more interesting and varied than my previous work at the Horak's, who only made use of my physical capabilities. Jan and his wife Lída were the proprietors and the shop sold better quality groceries and delicatessen items. One very popular brand of biscuits was McVitie's – there were about fifteen different selections on display. We also sold Swiss chocolate and sweets, Emmental and other cheeses, Slovakia's famous *bryndza,* a soft sheep's milk cheese, French mustard (which we used to buy in 200-litre barrels), sprats from Latvia, Russian caviar in tins, crab, lobster and many other items from England. We could only sell commodities which were listed for this type of business, which meant that we were not allowed to sell eggs, meat, vegetables or cigarettes. We were only allowed to sell fish at Christmas and then we kept live carp in barrels.

Right from the start I was taught to be precise in every aspect of the business and my work was regularly checked. Flour, sugar and other items were bought in bulk and stored in the cellar below our premises. These commodities had to be carefully weighed into 1-kg, ½-kg, and ¼-kg bags. The total weight had to tally too, as deficiencies, either spillages or overweighing had to come out of my pocket money. Quite simply, I was personally responsible for my mistakes. Mr. Matys' strict attitude made me very careful indeed.

Most of our stock was delivered to the shop but, on odd occasions and to get a better price, I had to take the handcart and collect items from a wholesaler or from the open market a few kilometres away. We sold four different brands of coffee, mostly Brazilian. To secure a better price when buying the unroasted coffee beans, Mr. Matys, Mr. Renda, Mr. Vinklárek and another grocer formed a small purchasing group. Once a fortnight we roasted and blended our own coffee at a special location, with a representative from each firm being present, usually an apprentice or an assistant. Most of the coffee was sold as coffee beans as nearly everyone had a coffee grinder at home. Our customers normally made monthly purchases, as they were mostly civil servants and were paid on a monthly basis.

In September I had to enrol at a half-day release school for apprentices. This was a compulsory two-year course, and the results had a great bearing on one's final qualifications as an assistant and for future employment. I also attended evening classes to learn how to arrange window displays.

In the autumn orders were taken for potatoes. Customers in our block had individual lock-up storage partitions in the cellar and this is where they kept their potatoes in winter. This used to be a big job. Potatoes were delivered to us in two batches of some fifty or sixty bags each and I had to carry them on my back to the customers. I soon developed some muscles and handling heavy loads did not seem to bother me any more. My monthly deliveries and the potato deliveries were usually reasonably well rewarded and, as this was my only source of income, I was very careful with the proceeds.

My father came to see Mrs. Matys and afterwards told me that I had passed my apprenticeship test. They also told him that they were very satisfied with my performance. It then became clear to me that, originally, I had only been accepted for a trial period. My father considered Mrs. Matys a very good person, sharing the same religion as ourselves and going to church twice every Sunday! To me, Mr. Matys, although I had to call him *Pan Šéf*, Mr Boss, was a very different person. In business he was very strict, in some cases unfair and even inhuman, but otherwise he was very humble and reasonable. And, on Sundays, he was unbelievably religious! On the whole, Mrs.

Matys was fair and kind, often protecting me from some of his outbursts on the business premises.

My accommodation in their house was rather modest but adequate. At mealtimes we all sat at the same table, even the maid. I had a great appetite and enjoyed their cooking, always eating everything I was given. I was tall, about 180 cm, nearly 6 ft, and still very thin.

At Christmas time business was very lively and there were many new articles on sale. These included *vánoční kolekce,* a special Christmas assortment of confectionery for hanging on a Christmas tree, and numerous varieties of other sweets and chocolates, Christmas decorations, Christmas trees, etc. The main dish on Christmas Eve was carp. We stocked live carp in barrels and it was my job to deliver them, in a bucket, to our customers on Christmas Eve. The fish was usually put in their bath and I would call back later to kill it. By 6 o'clock on Christmas Eve everything came to a halt. There was hardly any traffic about, the trains had stopped running, and so had the buses and most of the trams. Everyone tried to get home early in the evening to celebrate with their families. Later in the evening, it was quite common to attend a church service or mass.

New Years Eve, *Silvestr,* was usually celebrated by going to a dance, where the New Year would then be welcomed in. For good luck, you had to try and touch a chimney-sweep or a live piglet. These were both readily provided in the town for a small fee!

1935

I was making good progress at the half-day release school and Mr. Matys was informed accordingly. At work, I keenly grasped everything and became quite useful in every respect. Now and again I was given the keys to open up or even lock up the premises.

In the summer I was due for a holiday. Business was usually at its quietest, and arrangements were made and extra help hired for the duration of my absence. Holidays at home meant helping with the harvest, with work often starting at 5 in the morning and finishing very late at night. My parents were very pleased and proud that I had settled down so well in Bratislava. After having more than a year's experience of the big town of Bratislava, I felt quite superior to my friends from the nearby village of Bellova Ves.

When I returned to work, Mr. and Mrs. Matys went on their holidays, though one at a time. The presence of one of them was absolutely essential. Invariably, Mr. Matys went to Yugoslavia and Mrs. Matys to a Black Sea resort in Romania. Their daughter Lída was about three years old and during the holidays she was looked after by Mrs. Matys' mother who only lived a ten-minute walk away. In September I enrolled for my second year at the apprentice school and took an extra subject, book-keeping, at an evening class. I enjoyed these evening classes very much and I managed to make a number of new friends, if only for the duration of the course. My return home was strictly checked by Mr. Matys. By this time, on Sunday afternoons I was allowed to go out, but I had to be in church at six o'clock. If I had managed to save any money I would go to the cinema for the afternoon showing. Most of the films were English, some of them French, which meant that they were all subtitled.

At work, everything progressed nicely. Mr. Matys was even able to start learning English, while I attended to the customers. If no one was about he used to practice pronouncing the different 'th' sounds for days and days. His English tutor was the minister from our church, who also spoke English and had apparently studied in England. Mr. and Mrs. Matys also spoke very good German.

Our customers were mostly Czechs; however, there were also a few Slovaks. We also had quite a few professional soldiers – officers living in the same huge block of flats. The barracks were only a couple of kilometres away. The worst payers were often the wives of officers and I often had to go and ask to be paid for goods that I had delivered. Usually, this had to be done when their husbands were away on duty. I must have acquired some reasonable tact in these matters, because Mr. Matys invariably said "thank you"!

1936

I finished my apprenticeship schooling in June with excellent results. Mr. and Mrs. Matys were also very pleased with my results and quite often discussed them with our customers. Sometimes customers would discuss the problems they were having with their own children at school, most of whom attended the *gymnasium* – the grammar school, the *reálka* – the secondary school, or the commercial academy. I knew these children and, having received such an encouraging report from my apprentice school, I felt quite superior.

Now, when working in the shop, I was often left in charge during the slack periods and had to attend to everything. On rare occasions I was even entrusted to cash up. Being given this responsibility played an important part in my development and helped me gain confidence when speaking to other people. On Sunday afternoons, instead of going to the cinema, I started to take dancing lessons. These were held from 3.30 to 5.30. There were about 4 girls and 40 boys. It was great fun, as all of us had to learn from scratch. Eventually we made progress and could dance properly. I attended these classes for a whole year. My partner was a very good looking German girl, fairly tall, and after only a few lessons I was allowed to accompany her to her tram. I did not dare mention that I was taking dancing lessons or anything about the girl to Mr. and Mrs. Matys. And, without fail, I had to meet them at the church at 6.

This was the final year of my 3-year apprenticeship and it was coming to its close. But first, I had to pass my practical test prescribed by the *Gremium*, the Business Council. This consisted of visiting three different members of the *Gremium*, for half a day each, and performing normal duties in their shops. We were also asked questions about various commodities, methods of preparation, countries of origin, etc. Summaries of these tests were then sent to the *Gremium* to be judged. Only then would you receive your certificate to show that you had completed your apprenticeship – and qualify for promotion to 'Assistant'.

1937

Mr. and Mrs. Matys, not wanting to pay me an assistant's wage, had already started looking for another apprentice about three months before I qualified on 31st August. They were not successful in finding a suitable candidate and in the end they had to employ a qualified assistant. In the meantime, I had found myself a job through the Registered Assistant Office and started working as an assistant at *Delikatess K. Schuck* on Náměstí Republiky, right in the centre of Bratislava.

I lived in and was initially paid 300 crowns per month. For the first few months we lived in the 11-storey Manderla Building, known then as the Bratislava Skyscraper, and then close by in a flat, just a three minute walk from their business. It was a Jewish family delicatessen managed by Mr. and Mrs. K. Schmidt and their 17 year old son. There was also a cashier and another two assistants. The customers were very cosmopolitan and many of them were German and Hungarian. My knowledge of Hungarian from my home village was a great help. The proprietors spoke fluent German.

Foodstuffs sold at this delicatessen were much finer than the ones that I had been trained to handle. You could buy almost any imported item from anywhere in the world – Swiss cheeses and chocolates; Italian cheeses, mortadella and pasta; numerous brands of English packed teas and special biscuits; lobsters, crayfish, Portuguese sardines, Russian caviar, German pickled herrings; Hungarian salami (10 kg, 12 cm thick), Debrecín bacon and a great choice of French wines and Champagne. We used to boil our own legs of ham and slices were then sold on the premises in a roll of bread and served with a glass of wine. We also made our own salads – Russian, Italian, Swedish, etc – and various flavours of *bryndza*. This type of business certainly appealed to me and I learnt more and more every day.

The pre-Christmas rush started early, towards the end of November, and over 150 hampers had to be prepared and sent to recipients all over the country. It appeared to me as though our customers only worked in order to spend and spend, or perhaps this was my first encounter with people who could afford all these luxuries. On New Year's Day we were paid an extra month's wages in appreciation of our work.

1938

By early spring the business had slowed down considerably and, being the last one in, I had to look for another job. My apprenticeship, qualifications and recommendations were a great help, and the local Chamber of Trade where I was registered, found a job for me immediately.

On 1st April I started working for Mr. J. Karas, the proprietor of the Palace Hotel in Bratislava. He also had a delicatessen shop with an adjoining snack bar, open until midnight. I was accommodated in the Palace Hotel and shared a room with the hotel's chef. I acquired new experiences working as an assistant and a window dresser for the delicatessen items, and preparing a great variety of salads and aspic dishes. As this shop was open until midnight we also worked in shifts. I enjoyed this work very much, especially when working in the evenings.

Guests at our delicatessen restaurant were always very well dressed – perhaps they were on their way to a concert hall, a cinema, a theatre, a show or a cabaret. Seeing all this going on around me gave me the inspiration and desire to educate myself even more and improve my status. To assess my prospects I got in touch with Professor Pečeňka, who had been my teacher at the day release school for the apprentices. (He used to give extra lessons there; his main teaching post was at the Commercial Academy.) Professor Pečeňka explained what I would have to do and thought that my qualifications would be sufficient to take the entrance exams. However, it was up to me to get acquainted with the actual requirements.

I borrowed lots of books from my friends who were already at the Academy and asked for their help and guidance. I had to catch up on four years of absence from school and I found it very hard indeed; there was so much to take in, in preparation for my entry exams. About three days before my exams I came to a point when I could just not learn anymore, and my mind went blank. My exams were at the end of June and lasted for two days. To my great surprise, about 14 days later I was informed that I had passed and was accepted to enrol for my first year at the Commercial Academy.

This meant that at nearly 19 years of age I had committed myself to four years of college studies. I now informed my employer about my success and he was kind enough to keep me in his service until the very last day before starting at the Academy. After the exams, I had gone home for the weekend and told my parents all about my intentions. They accepted my decision, although with mixed feelings, as I was earning well and also had some savings. I only asked to be able to live at home and promised to pay for my enrolment and purchase all the books out of my savings. Mother and Father, seeing my determination, consented.

My parents were going to move again, this time to Kotelszer Pusta, a small farming settlement just over 3 km from Biskupice Pri Dunaji[6], just south of Bratislava; about half an hour by train followed by a good half hour's walk. Ludvík had just come home after completing his national service in the army, where he had become a sergeant, and Jaroslav had just started his national service. My sister Božena and her husband Richard Koubek now lived next door to us in

---

[6] Now Podunajské Biskupice

a terraced worker's cottage and had helped our parents with all the work in the forest and the fields, especially when Ludvík had been called up for national service.

Early in September I started to attend my new college in Bratislava, walking or cycling every morning to catch my train. At the college I soon made new friends, most of them, however, from higher classes. My very close friends were Alfred Kellner, a Hungarian, and J. Ganobčík, a Slovak. Both finished their course successfully and were awarded their engineering degrees.

Initially I had to work hard to keep up with the syllabus, often taking lessons and tuition from my friends and arriving home on later trains. All the lessons in college were in Slovak although many of the books had been published by Czech professors. We also had to learn two foreign languages: I chose German and English. A few of the professors were Czech but they had to teach in Slovak. A Slovak nationalist movement had been formed with German support, resulting in some very unpleasant scenes, discrimination, etc. Czechs were accused of exploiting the Slovaks, and demands were made for all Czechs to leave Slovakia. The status of our family was interpreted differently, as we had come to Slovakia from Russia. I was fluent in Slovak and had no problems at the college, although everyone knew that I was Czech. Being the oldest, I was elected class monitor for the year.

In Bohemia and Moravia the situation had become very critical. The country had been forced to surrender large areas of Bohemia and Moravia, the Sudetenland, to the Germans at the beginning of October. My brother Ludvík was called up again and served in the artillery regiment in Bratislava. During this national emergency, I also volunteered to join the army. However, being too young, I was told that my year group was not yet required.

In the meantime, Slovakia had achieved a considerable degree of autonomy and was managing its part of the country independently, except for foreign affairs and the army. Internal squabbles and intrigues led to many blunders. However, aspirations to become a free state, as a Slovak nation, were supported by a small section of the public and some extremists and, with German help, they eventually succeeded in creating a puppet Slovak Republic.

1939

On 15th March German forces occupied the remaining parts of Bohemia and Moravia. On the previous day, Slovakia had been forced by the Germans to proclaim their independence as a Free Slovak state, or face partial annexation and occupation of the remaining areas by Hungary and Poland. After these events large numbers of Czechs left Slovakia, some voluntarily, some forcibly. At college, there were only a few small changes. Most of the staff were Slovaks and the few Czechs who were still there were indispensable. The new head of the college was Professor Ursiny.

Official news from Bohemia and Moravia was almost non-existent. At first, the only source was via the 'jungle telegraph'. A few weeks later all the atrocities of the annexation were confirmed by escapees who had managed to get away from the clutches of the Gestapo. News from abroad offered good moral support and we listened daily to foreign broadcasts late at night, when there was least interference on our battery radios. However, nobody could understand why we had been sacrificed to the Germans and why no one, in the East or West, was willing to help us.

From the end of June, after having successfully passed my first year exams at college, I stayed at home for two months to help with the harvest. Ludvík was demobbed in July. There were many conflicting pieces of news about the events in Bohemia and Moravia, about persecution, imprisonments, people disappearing, underground movements, escape routes, etc. We also learnt about the establishment of a base in Krakow, Poland, for those who were willing to fight against the Germans.

Although he had been working very hard during the harvest, Ludvík managed to disappear at night on many occasions. However, he refused to divulge anything about these activities to anyone. Towards the end of August he disappeared for four days and we were all terribly worried. On his brief reappearance we learnt that he had been to Krakow, illegally making his way by foot over the High Tatra Mountains and, according to what he told us, had been sent back to Bratislava with a message. After packing a few things he left home late at night on 29th August with the words, "The less you know, the better for all concerned". However, I was taken into his confidence and was given the address of a Mr. A. Baláš, his best friend from the army, where I could leave any information of military value, for instance, about the transit of armoured forces, personnel, unusual activities, etc.

On 1st September 1939, Germany invaded Poland.

Our house in Hviezdoslavov

The farm at Nagy Hegy

My rabbit hutches, 1932

Harvest time at Kotelszer Pusta, 1934

Harvest time at Kotelszer Pusta, 1934

Family photograph, 1931. From left to right; Jaroslav, Marie, Emilie, myself, Božena, Pavel, Růžena and Ludvík

Chapter 3: Czechoslovakia II

1939 September – December
I commenced my second year at college early in September. Again, I was elected class monitor. Our form master was Professor I. Svozil, a Czech who had spent many years teaching in Slovakia and who had written several books in Slovak, which were currently used at the college. At home, whilst listening to all the news we always wondered whether Ludvík had managed to survive and was safe somewhere. Jaroslav was still in the army somewhere in Slovakia. We had very little news from him.

On a few occasions, I was able to pass on information to my contact, thinking it may be of some military value. We also took precautions and arranged secret signals for our next meeting, as he thought he was being watched. Through friends and people I knew in Bratislava, news started to reach us of the persecutions in Bohemia and Moravia, especially of army and air force personnel. Consequently, many of them had gone into hiding and were on the run, trying to get to France via Yugoslavia. I was approached by two bank managers in Bratislava (like our family, they were members of the Czech Brethren) and was asked if I could organize an escape route through the area where we lived. Kotelszer Pusta was close to the Danube, and only 3½ km from the new Hungarian border. The town of Šamorín, about 10 km away, was already in Hungarian hands.

In a very short time I was able to organize an escape route with the help of the Czechs who had been kept on in various key positions. The Slovaks had no one to replace them and among them were stationmasters, teachers, the head of the local *četník* station and some others who were married to Slovaks. At first, my task seemed quite an adventure and I was very proud of being involved in such a noble cause. I had full backing from my parents and that was the greatest support I could have. In the evenings, while the weather was still reasonably good, I was able to accompany parties of up to eight people, partly by train and partly on foot, and bring them to within about 400 m of the Hungarian borders. I instructed them where to cross, where to go and what to say when purchasing their train tickets for Budapest. The bank managers in Bratislava provided them with Hungarian currency. By December my extra activities had begun to affect my course work, and on quite a few occasions I was absent from college. Without going into any great detail, I approached my form master, Professor Svozil, and he was very sympathetic to my reasons for being absent so often; perhaps he had already guessed about my involvement.

Jaroslav was demobbed in the middle of December. However, being Czech, he was sent to Moravia, which was now occupied by the Germans. Only after he had managed to convince the authorities there that his parents lived in Slovakia and that our domicile was in Slovakia, was he allowed to come home, arriving a few days before Christmas.

His mind was already made up. On Boxing Day, and taking only an attaché case, I escorted him to the Hungarian border. After producing his original domicile papers, which confirmed that he was still a resident in Štvrtok Na Ostrove, now occupied by the Hungarians, the border guard let him pass without delay. I went back home alone and had to explain his disappearance; he had left without even saying goodbye. My parents were heartbroken and implored me not to leave them without prior warning, as they would like to give me their blessing. Jaroslav was able to make his way to Veľký Lég, from where he took a train to Budapest. He eventually reached Marseilles, travelling via Turkey and Beirut.

News reached us from Hungary confirming that many of the Czechs who had been caught at the border were immediately put in prison and some were even sent back to the Slovak authorities. As there was no other way to get to Yugoslavia, except through Hungary, we had to take immediate steps on our side and brief everyone in great detail about the journey, crossing the border, buying railway tickets, and even teach everyone a few words of Hungarian.

The winter was severe with a lot of snow and this became an additional hazard. Many of the escapees became exhausted and suffered from frostbitten feet. Sometimes, up to ten people stayed at our house for a whole week because of the bad weather and deep snow. My brother-in-law, Richard Koubek, now became my main support, especially when it came to taking people right up to the border from our home.

1940 January

In January I was able to establish another escape route through Miloslavov, 8 km from where we lived. The escape route was in a slightly different direction but the train route was almost the same. Karol Vaculík, who lived in Miloslavov, was able to help me on numerous occasions to get the people across the border.

As we were taking people across the border in winter, I realised how easily we could be spotted by the border guards. My idea of introducing some sort of white cape was accepted. Money was provided for this purpose and my mother soon made dozens of them. Initially, we accompanied the groups all the way across the borders, bringing back the capes. However, it was soon realised that it was better to let them keep the capes and get away the same night, as far as possible from the crossing points.

In February, I received a message through my contact, who was a friend of the head of the Slovak border guards, that I should ease off on my activities, as there were a few guards who had been posted to his station who could not be trusted. I had to change the method of transportation and, instead of travelling by train, I arranged for them to use buses or even taxis and then complete their journey to our house on foot. Fortunately, my father was often able to meet us with horses and sledges. In Bratislava, my accomplices thought that we should take the warning given by our border guard contact very seriously and one weekend towards the end of January I was sent to eastern Slovakia to establish another escape route, near Košice. Although I managed to do this, we were soon betrayed by a new and enthusiastic border guard.

My position in this illegal underground work was appraised by my friends and it was decided that I, too, would soon have to leave the country. I was to make my way to Budapest and then try to establish a new route for our people so that they could travel safely through Hungary. My contact in Budapest was a bank executive, Mr. Šalek. Knowing that I was shortly going to leave the country, I asked my form master to hear me out. I spent almost an hour with him and seeing my determination to pursue what I considered was my duty, he gave me his blessing. So as not to cause any problems at college because of my absence, I wrote a letter to the head of the college, informing him that I had had to leave due to domestic problems at home.

February

By the beginning of February, the growing numbers of people who were running away from the German occupation and persecution became quite a problem for us. We were forced to find temporary accommodation in Bratislava. A few Czech and some Slovak families helped to ease the strain. The penalties for harbouring escapees were severe. Slovak nationalists and some enthusiastic members of their police force had to be reckoned with. One day, while I was discussing problems of accommodation and feeding people in Bratislava with Mr. Knobloch, a bank manager, in his office, a man burst in crying: "Quickly, you've got to save me, the police are after me". He gave the right password and we were able to help him. I exchanged my winter coat for his blue Air Force coat – he was a pilot – and made him memorize an address and how he could get there without getting into any further trouble. I also managed to leave quickly through the back door of the manager's office. At home, my parents were surprised to see me in a military coat; my explanation was that someone had preferred my coat!

Our neighbours at Kotelszer Pusta were also farmers – Mr. Ančik lived together with his brother Zdeněk and his wife Marta. They were all quite willing to help us, especially during the later stages, contributing to share the burden of feeding the escapees. On one or two occasions Zdeněk volunteered to take escapees en route to Šamorín to the border.

My time at home was running out. My ever-increasing activities, guiding escapees and making frequent journeys to the border, must have been noticed by the border guards. I had to make preparations for my own escape. This time, my parents fully understood the situation and gave me their blessing. In Bratislava, all the members of our illegal group, which included the bank managers, helped make plans for the next steps to be taken on my arrival in Budapest. I was given a name, Mr. Šalek, and the address of another bank manager in Budapest who would advise me about the local conditions and other aspects of our illegal activities. Our intention was to improve the transit conditions for the escapees, and especially for those travelling through Šamorín, after they had left our house. For instance, we knew that the language barrier created numerous problems, even when purchasing railway tickets to Budapest or another town. I was also asked to report about the news that had reached us in Bratislava concerning the treatment of escapees in Hungary and problems of leaving the country, even when help had been offered by the French consulate on Fö Utca (Main Street) in Budapest.

A friend of mine, J. Černil, the son of a stationmaster, eventually passed on a warning, which was not unexpected, to leave the country within two days. The day I was going to leave, our neighbour ZdeněkAnčik decided to join me. He was about twice my age and could not speak a word of Hungarian. On 19th February we set out from home. This time, however, we were taken to the border by my father on a sledge. My mother's last words were: "If I were younger, I would also go with you."

At the border, my father started to worry about our plans. How were we going to get to Šamorín without passports or other papers? All I had was a bankbook with a written note in Slovak requesting that I be allowed to call at the bank and straighten out the terms regarding some repayments. The bank book belonged to my father and I was going to be acting on his behalf, with Zdeněk as my adviser. I also told the border guards that I was going to visit the family where I lodged in 1930 while attending secondary school. (The head of this family later became a very well-known personality.) After about half an hour, the officers in charge of the crossing, having consulted with their headquarters, allowed us to proceed to Šamorín. I waved to my father and said good-bye. Unknown to me then, it would be more than five years before I saw him or my mother again.

After three quarters of an hour's walk we reached the military HQ and went to report, as instructed by the border guards. There I was given the new address of my landlord from 1930. We were allowed to stay in Šamorín until 12 noon the next day and reported again to the military HQ. So far so good, my knowledge of Hungarian was a great asset.

I went to visit my former landlord on my own. Although he was bed-ridden and extremely ill, he was still very delighted to see me. I had to explain the purpose of my visit and he understood that it was serving as a cover-up for our real intentions. He also gave us the name and address of a farm where we could stay for the night and where they would also provide a horse and sledge to take us to Dunajská Streda, en route to Budapest. We had to pay the farmer quite a large sum for these services. The winter conditions were very bad indeed. Halfway to Dunajská Streda the farmer said that he did not want to go any further because of the blizzard. With the help of a few extra *pengő*[7] we pushed on. Two or three times we were stopped by *četníks*, in their typical feathered hats, and they accepted the farmer's explanations that we were all going to visit friends. Zdeněk had to pretend that he was fast asleep. He was well wrapped up, lying down at the rear end of the sledge.

By this time we expected that the military authorities would have notified all the *četníks* and a search for us would have been started. We were very lucky and reached Dunajská Streda undetected. My father had given me the address of a Jewish merchant who used to buy our corn when we lived in Nagy Hegy. As I had attended secondary school here, I knew my way about. I soon found the merchant and called to see him early in the evening. At his door I explained what the visit was all about and he nearly panicked. Not knowing what to do, he quickly took me to their kitchen and explained the predicament that he himself was in. A Hungarian army officer was billeted in one of his rooms and I would have to leave as quickly as possible without being noticed as they were orthodox Jews and my appearance would not fit in. However, he gave me the address of his empty warehouse, a wooden shed with a concrete floor, where we could stay the night and promised to bring us some *slivovice* and a sandwich at midnight. He kept his word and we were most grateful, as we hadn't eaten for a long time. It was so cold in the warehouse that we had to keep walking about all the time. He begged us to leave and not to come back, as he was in great danger of losing everything he owned if he was found harbouring escapees. We said that we would leave early in the morning.

We kept our promise and at about five o'clock in the morning we left for the railway station, hoping to find somewhere warm to wait. We were unlucky; the railway station didn't open until six and we had to keep walking about to keep warm. We returned to the station and bought our tickets for Budapest. About a quarter of an hour before the train was due to depart there were so many *četníks* and military personnel about that we decided not to stay around in such a confined area. Later, when we had boarded the train, we soon discovered that our plan to sit next to each other wouldn't work – the train was packed. Not being able to answer a single word, Zdeněk had to

---

[7] Hungarian currency, 1927 - 1946

pretend that he had a sore throat and couldn't speak. Eventually I was able to swap seats and calm him down a little. The *četniks* came through the train twice, as if they were looking for someone, but we managed to survive the ordeal.

About half way through our journey, an old school friend of mine saw me and came over for a chat. We had attended the secondary school in Dunajská Streda together and he still lived there. His mother was Hungarian and he thought that we had stayed on and now lived under the Hungarians. I did not correct him, hoping that he would vouch for us if there was an identity check en route, as we did not have any valid papers. I told him that I was intending to find a job in Budapest and that my neighbour Zdeněk was just accompanying me. We parted company at the railway station in Budapest and I promised to come and visit him some time in Dunajská Streda.

I then started to follow the instructions I had been given in order to reach my contact, Mr. Šalek, in Budapest. I gave a taxi driver an address only to find out that that particular house had been demolished and it was just an empty site. This was not a good way to cover my tracks! However, we were not very far from our actual destination and, while Zdeněk walked up and down the street, I went to ring Mr. Šalek's door bell. Giving the password and introducing myself frightened Mrs. Šalek so much that she started to cry. After hearing from her that the secret police had taken her husband away only the day before and that their flat may be under surveillance, I quickly departed. I then met up again with Zdeněk, who had been walking around for about twenty minutes on the opposite side of the street, as prearranged.

Our next move was to try and get to the French Consulate on Fö Utca. This time we decided to walk, as we couldn't trust any of the taxi drivers. For more than half an hour we walked back and forth along the road opposite the French Consulate, studying every detail of their entrance door so that we could make a quick entry. A Hungarian policeman was on duty, patrolling up and down outside the consulate.

When he reached the furthest point from the entrance we quickly crossed the street but found, to our horror, that we couldn't open the door. We nearly panicked and then the policeman came slowly towards us and, without saying a single word, turned the knob and let us in! After travelling for a whole day, with tension mounting all the time and then a series of disappointments, we thought that we would now be able to relax a little. We were wrong – five men sitting at a table close to the lift on the ground floor started to question us, trying to find out who we were and about our intentions. These men formed some sort of liaison group between escapees and the French Consulate. They also gathered information about the credibility of the escapees, arranged accommodation and organized transport and escape routes to Yugoslavia. After our debriefing, we were sent to safe accommodation. At this point I parted with Zdeněk as I was billeted at a different address, 14 Kiraly Utca. We were not given any papers at the consulate and our presence and activities in Hungary were still highly illegal, and it would have been very dangerous for us if we had been confronted in any way.

The report about me calling at the French Consulate must have reached the higher echelons of our organisation in Budapest because, about two days later, Dr. Kalanová called to see me and I was able to pass on some important information to her. This included requests from our underground movement in Bratislava as well as my report about my visit to Mr. Šalek's home and his arrest. Her husband, Mr. Kalan, worked at the Yugoslavian Consulate in Budapest. After a long discussion with her, it was easier for me to understand the predicament we were in with regard to all escapees. Our misgivings about the way those Czechs who were trying to find a way to reach Yugoslavia, were being treated in Hungary were confirmed. Anyone apprehended at the border or anywhere in Hungary was immediately imprisoned. Some were sent back to Slovakia after three or four weeks in prison. Most of the military personnel were held in the Citadel, an old stone fortress on Gellért-hegy, Gellert Hill, in central Budapest.

Because of my knowledge of Hungarian, I was asked to stay in Budapest and stay in touch with our liaison group at the French Consulate. A message was sent to our escape group organizers about the prevailing conditions in Hungary and about my new mission in Budapest. My first assignment was to continue doing the same job as my predecessors, Erwin and Mudroch, who had now become rather well-known and were familiar faces in the town, and who could have been picked up at any time by the Hungarian secret police. I had two tasks: to take the escapees from the consulate to safe accommodation, willingly provided by the Jewish community, and to pay the flat owners, at a per-person per-day rate, every third or fourth day.

Due to some mishap, one of our established escape routes, via Nagykanizsa, had to be abandoned for a few days. A new link had to be set up and put into operation again, as there were far too many people waiting in our safe houses. I was sent to Nagykanizsa to contact a Mr. Farago, a Hungarian with whose help we were then able to open up the route again. On top of my work in Budapest I also became a guide again, taking people with me via this escape route to Nagykanizsa. Here I handed them over to a Hungarian who in turn arranged for them to be ferried by rowing boat across the River Drava to Yugoslavia. I used to take ten to fourteen people in one go, pretending that I was in charge of a group of sportsmen, holding all their tickets and doing all the talking with the conductor on the train.

On a few occasions in Budapest, Dr. Kalanová and I went to the gates of the Citadel to meet some of our politicians and high-ranking officers through the offices of the Red Cross. In groups of six, and in one group per day, Citadel prisoners were allowed to go to one of the city's bathing houses. They were trusted on their honour. Knowing the exact times of these comings and goings we were able to meet them near the gates and pass on necessities, such as toiletries, which had been approved by the Red Cross. More important, however, was that we could start planning their escape from the Citadel.

March

Because their appeals for help to heads of states, the Pope and many world organizations did not yield any response, the situation, especially in central Europe and the Balkans was fragile and explosive. There was even talk that the Gestapo was already in Budapest and that all the escapees in the Citadel would be handed over to the Germans. At that time almost one hundred Czechs were detained in the Citadel. Preparations for a mass escape of the Czech detainees were in their final stages (Professor Nigrin, Lt.Col. Sklenovský, and others). The break-out was to take place on Saturday, 30th March. My task was to arrange the transport, i.e. lorries and taxis. However, my last meeting planned with Dr. Kalanová, when she was going to pass on money and my final instructions, did not take place. Instead, on Wednesday, 27th March, I took fourteen escapees to Nagykanizsa, en route to Yugoslavia.

Returning late in the evening to my lodgings at 14 Kiraly Utca, I was apprehended by the secret police, who were there waiting for me.

After a brief interrogation, which was conducted in Slovak, I was taken away in their car. Before we reached their HQ they stopped and searched another three houses – obviously they were in possession of addresses of our illegal safe houses. Later I learned that the owner of one of the flats, Mr. Klein, had confessed when interrogated by police regarding an incident in connection with harbouring escapees. After some rough treatment he gave the police a few more addresses. It appears that I was the only victim of his disclosure. (We did, however, manage to move people elsewhere when Mr. Klein was detained.)

My attempt to bribe the driver of the police car with my watch, which he had admired so much, did not work and we reached their HQ close to midnight. I was put in an iron cage, only about three by four metres, along with another forty or fifty detainees – it was strictly standing room only! As I was most probably the youngest among them and a foreigner, they were very sympathetic. However, some of them pointed out to me that there was not much justice in Hungary and that I should not expect any mercy.

The following day in the evening, four secret policemen started to interrogate me. They tried to conduct the proceedings in Hungarian, but I did not respond. Right from the very beginning I claimed to speak Slovak only. My blue Czech Air Force great coat, which I had acquired in Bratislava while helping one of the escapees, created some doubt in their minds as to my total innocence that I fervently claimed. I only admitted that I had come to Hungary illegally and that I was hoping to reach Yugoslavia and eventually get to France. They wanted to know every detail about how I had managed to get to Budapest. I stuck to one story, without disclosing any associations with anyone else and without admitting any knowledge of any name in Bratislava or in Budapest. Their method of interrogation soon changed. At first, I was slapped in my face a few times. As this did not yield any further results, I was tied up by my wrists and made to clasp my hands over my shins. A broomstick was then pushed through under my knees, effectively locking me in a crouching position. My shoes were taken off and they started beating me on my bare soles and bottom. This lasted for a considerable time. Twice, after passing out, they had to pour water on to my face to revive me. But I just stuck to the same story. After yet another beating I was left lying, still tied in a bundle, on the floor while they all went into an adjoining room to consult with their commander.

This time my knowledge of Hungarian paid off. I overheard most of their conversation about how they were going to continue their interrogation. I was to get another severe beating and if this did not make me admit anything further then it was the commander's opinion that I was either too young and innocent of any serious crime, or just damn clever. My last beating was administered with such severity that it was impossible afterwards to stand on my feet. Two uniformed policemen held me under my arms and walked me up and down the room to stop my legs from swelling. I was then taken to a different prison, Hadik, and two days later I was transferred to the Maria Terezia military barracks for solitary confinement. I was very frightened and wondered whether they were going to find out more about my activities. These were perhaps the most desperate days of my imprisonment.

After about seven days I was moved to a civilian prison, Toloncz Haz. This was a very welcome sign. I could now relax and plan my next steps. There were quite a few Czech escapees here, about sixty in all, including Lt. Jilma (later to become a general in Russia) and Major Reda, a veterinary doctor who had stayed at our house in Slovakia before crossing the border into Hungary. Members of our mission at the French Consulate, as well as others working for the same cause, and the Red Cross were in reasonably regular contact with us. They were able to bribe the prison authorities and arrange for our expulsion from Hungary quite quickly.

April

On 18th April I was sent by train, with eleven other escapees, to Košice in eastern Slovakia. The town was then under Hungarian rule, and we spent a day in the local military jail. It was an unforgettable experience – because of the bugs! They were certainly after my blood! The following day, late in the afternoon, we set out under military escort, four soldiers, towards the Slovak border which was about 6 km north of the town centre. It was a dark afternoon and the ground was wet. About half way to our destination we overtook an old gentleman with a stick who spoke Slovak, and he passed a quick message to us. It was an address we could go to, if we managed to get back to Košice. We walked on until we were about 200 m from the Slovak border and the Slovak border guards. The Hungarian guards ordered us to proceed, holding their rifles at the ready. We were trapped. To our left was an open space and a railway track and, to our right, quite a steep wooded hill. We all decided to scatter into the hillside and take cover among the trees. There was a lot of shouting from the border guards on both sides but not a single shot was fired. Three of us, including a Czech pilot, decided to stick together.

After an all night march through the woods and over the hills, we managed to get back to Košice at around 5 a.m. We split up again and kept a reasonable distance apart to avoid being apprehended by the police. Our shoes and trousers were in a very bad state and we were lucky not to meet anyone at all. We found the address that the old gentleman had given us. Mr. Pavelka was a publican, and I think that he was also a Slovak, working for our cause and also for the Polish Red Cross. After a good meal and a bath, and after cleaning and drying our clothes, we had a short rest. Early in the afternoon he bought us train tickets and we were again on our way to Budapest. Unfortunately, we had not heard that anyone else had made it back to Košice.

The publican warned us not to go directly to the French Consulate on arrival. We were told that the Consulate was now being watched very closely. We were given an alternative address, where we could enquire about our next steps in Budapest. There was only one person at this new address. He urged us to disappear quietly, and gave us another safer address where we could stay the night. The situation in Budapest was very tense as many of our safe houses had been raided by the secret police and a few people had been caught and imprisoned again. All the people I had known before my arrest as well as those at the French Consulate (Hanák, Kralík, Roby and Malý) and other contacts, including Dr. Kalanová, had had to escape to Yugoslavia.

On 21st April I was given a new task – to guide and accompany a group of eleven escapees via Nagykanizsa and on to Yugoslavia. Having used this route for escapees a few times before, it was almost a routine mission and I was especially happy knowing that I too would be going to Yugoslavia. We arrived in Nagykanizsa without a hitch. I knew our contact there from my previous work. We carefully spread out and followed him to a café where we sat in twos and threes, pretending not to know one other. After a brief consultation with my Hungarian contact our plans had to be changed due to a mishap the previous night when someone had been shot on the banks of the River Drava while trying to escape. On this route, the only way we could get to Yugoslavia was by boat, which could carry six people at a time. The River Drava was very fast flowing and, at our crossing point, about 80 m wide.

The river's northern bank was in Hungary and its southern bank in Yugoslavia. It was continually patrolled by motorboats fitted with searchlights. We were taken to a safe house, where we had to wait until the following day for further news from our contact. Most of the escapees in this group were strangers to each other and having been given this unexpected opportunity, when all they could do was wait, people opened up and discussed freely their past lives and their intentions and hopes for their future. Most of them had been in active military service, as officers or NCOs, and others were civilians with their National Service years behind them. I was the youngest and had not even been called up. During these discussions everybody readily gave their rank and the unit they had served with, and when they had done their national service. There was, however, one man, Reich, about 35 years old, who was very unwilling to tell us anything about himself. His national service and call-up dates during the Czech Emergency in 1938 did not tally. He was unable to tell us the names of the officers in charge of the units he had supposedly served in. He said he had forgotten. We were all very uneasy and worried about the situation. Nobody wanted to deal with the matter and we pretended not to be too serious about it, as our chances of getting to Yugoslavia were still a bit slim.

On the following day, 22nd April, our contact came for us at 10 p.m. and took us in two cars to an empty house about half a kilometre from the River Drava – the border. He was going to take us to the boats at midnight. First, he checked the movements of the border guards' patrol boat and also made sure that our boats were ready for our crossing. The house where we were waiting was only lit by candles, one in each of the two rooms. Some of us were wondering whether our contact would bring the police and take us all back to Budapest and prison!

Plans were discussed about what we were to do should this happen. Some were very daring and said that they would swim across the river. More serious plans were discussed, very quietly, about Reich, who just did not fit in. Finally, a decision was made to dispose of him while crossing the river. Two strong men were chosen to stick by him on leaving the safe house and see to the rest when we were half-way across the river. To our astonishment, about fifteen minutes before we were due to leave the house, he said: "Listen all of you. I know you all are feeling very uneasy about me. I am not going with you, and I am not going to report you to the police either. I only wanted to find out if any Poles were going with you or you were in any way integrated with their underground movement." He then opened the door and left.

Tension was eased when our contact came as promised at midnight. We followed him like geese all the way down to the river but to our dismay there was only one boat. One group of six went across immediately and it took almost an hour before the boat came back for the last five of us. In the meantime we hid behind the bushes on the river bank, while a patrol boat went up and down the river twice, aiming its searchlight along the shores. At about 1.30 a.m. on 23rd April, I crossed the River Drava. At last, I had reached Yugoslavia.

Our intention was to get as far as possible inland, away from the border, as we were not quite sure about the latest developments in Yugoslavia. Our worries and problems were instantly solved when a Yugoslav border guard shouted *stoj*, halt, and asked me who I was. After saying that I was Czech, the guard put his rifle on his back, came over to me and embraced me, welcoming me to Yugoslavia. Using a single prearranged whistle, I was able to assemble all the men from our second boat and we were taken to the guard room for refreshments and drinks – raising a toast to our brotherly friendship.

In the morning we were taken to Terezino Polje, a small settlement right on the river bank, and waited in the pub for further instructions. By lunchtime all the necessary formalities had been completed and we proceeded to Virovitica, where we boarded the train for Zagreb. Although we were free, we were asked not to attract unnecessary attention from the rest of the public, because Yugoslavia also had its own political problems. On our arrival, late in the afternoon, in Zagreb, we were welcomed by Lt. Jaromír Hlubík, who was acting on behalf of the Czechoslovak Military Mission in Belgrade, and by Professor Smetánka of the Czechoslovak House Club, which was used as a liaison centre for Czech escapees.

We were billeted at the Czechoslovak House Club in Zagreb. The following day, after a brief interrogation by Lt. Hlubík, the rest of the group was sent to Belgrade, with the highest ranking officer in charge of the transport. However, the Czechoslovak Military Mission wanted me to stay on in Zagreb and await further instructions. In a very short time, Lt. Hlubík and I became very good friends, especially when we realised that we had been linked to the same escape route a few months back, helping to get people out of Czechoslovakia.

May

After about two weeks I was sent back to the border, this time, however, to act on the Yugoslav side as a replacement for Alois Kasel, who had then gone on to Belgrade. I became a liaison officer, liaising between the Czechoslovak Military Mission and the Yugoslav civil and military authorities in the region between Terezino Polje and Virovitica. My task was to minimize the work and problems for the Yugoslavs and to organize proper control over the escapees reaching this part of Yugoslavia, issuing each one with a travel document which would suffice if there were police checks on the trains. All escapees in this region were brought to me by the border guards. After interrogating them briefly, I sent them on to Zagreb to contact Lt. Hlubík. Among the many I interviewed were Lt.Col. Karel Klapálek, Major Střelka, Major Kobliha, and Staff Captain Zástěra. A summary of my interviews was sent with the appointed leader of each transport to Zagreb.

I was given a room in a pub situated about 200 m from the bridge over the River Drava to Hungary, and this served as my sleeping quarters and office. Many of the border guards used to come to the pub when off duty or in between their shifts. This gave me the opportunity to treat them to a drink and offer them cigarettes. During this time on the Yugoslav-Hungarian border I used to smoke about forty or fifty cigarettes a day, 'politely' smoking with everyone to retain a friendly atmosphere. As I was neither a drinker nor a smoker, I had quite a problem trying to keep up with my hardened comrades.

The Poles also had a liaison officer here, Karczewski, and they came in much greater numbers as the Hungarians were quite friendly towards them. However, the Yugoslavs did not show them the same kindness. This was because the Poles had been prepared to take Těšín by force from Czechoslovakia during the 1938 crisis.*

*For details of Czech-Polish border problems in 1938 and the expulsion of the Czechs, see *My Struggle for Freedom* by Josef Novák, published by Melandrium Books.

On two or three occasions I was asked to visit Mr Pavlát, the head of police in the district, who wanted to know if there were any problems regarding military or police co-operation in his area. I was taken to see him in a police car and certainly felt very important. I shall never forget the Yugoslav people – civilians as well as members of the military and police forces – for their brotherly treatment and the way they looked after us.

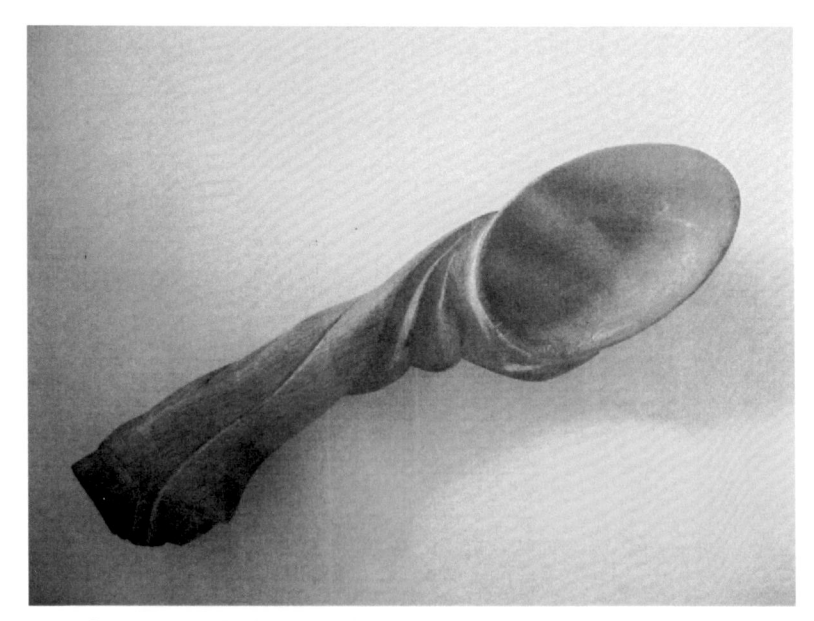

Wooden spoon fashioned from a coat hanger, given to me by another prisoner while in Toloncz Haz prison

On our train journey through Turkey

Chapter 4: Middle East

1940 June
By the beginning of June the influx of Czechoslovak escapees was beginning to slow down. The Hungarian police were tightening their security and it became increasingly more difficult to travel anywhere without some sort of documents. Consequently, the route I was operating had to be abandoned. The bad news of the fighting in France and also of the uncertain future of Yugoslavia contributed to my early recall from the border. On 14th June I returned to Zagreb and helped Lt. Hlubík obliterate all traces of the escapees who had been temporarily billeted in the Czechoslovak House in Zagreb. On 20th June we reported to Staff Captain Selner and Lt. Štětka at the Czechoslovak Military Mission in Beograd. Marta Ančíková, the wife of Zdeněk Ančik, our neighbour in Slovakia, was there too.

On 21st June, I and many others received our travel documents from the French Consulate and we were told to be ready for a quick departure to Beirut, then under the French Mandate for Syria and the Lebanon. As our only possessions comprised a tooth brush, toothpaste and a towel given to us the day before, we did not have much of a problem packing.

On the 24th June about fifty of us departed from Beograd under the command of Lt.Col. Klapálek. During the night, en route through Yugoslavia, we made a couple of stops when local Czechs came to bid us farewell and wish us a speedy return to our homeland. Their food parcels were very much appreciated, as we did not have any extra food or even money in reserve.

On the morning of 25th June we crossed into Greece. To my surprise, at the first border stop I saw border guards in their national costume and could hardly imagine them as serving soldiers. We arrived in Salonika in the evening and crossed the border into Turkey, reaching Istanbul on 26th June and sleeping at a hotel for the night. In the morning we went sightseeing, looking at the Suleiman mosque, the harbour and the fortifications. Everything was so different, so oriental and very busy. A ferry took us across the Bosphorus to Asia Minor and then we continued by train to Ankara. After a short stop, we proceeded through the snowy Taurus Mountains. The countryside of Turkey was poor; homes looked dilapidated and were made of inadequate materials. The fields seemed to be neglected and I wondered how people managed to make a living. Only their towns give the impression of civilized existence: the buildings were constructed of better materials, commerce was livelier and there were functioning transport systems.

We crossed the borders into Syria and reached Aleppo on 28th June. There was no opportunity to see anything, except from the train. We could only catch a glimpse of the fortified Citadel. Now we were all anxious to get to Beirut and proceed quickly to France. Not hearing any news about how the war in France was developing, our only thoughts were with those lucky ones who were fighting in France. We really wanted to join them and in particular I wanted to meet up with my brother Jaroslav, who had passed through Beirut four months previously. At last we arrived in Beirut, on 29th June, and were accommodated in the French military barracks. We were given blankets and food and were treated as military personnel. That meant that we were also entitled to wine. The barracks were situated just outside the city on high ground.

News of the fighting in France was now reaching us almost continually during the day. We were told that there would be no more boats to take us to France where the situation now looked desperate. France had capitulated and our presence in Beirut became dangerous, as the Germans insisted that the Lebanese border be closed to all traffic. The French military authorities somehow managed to by-pass these orders and transport our group, sixteen of us in all, including Lt.Col. Klapálek, along with others who were still in Beirut, into Palestine. On 3rd July we arrived at Camp Az-Sumeiriya a few miles south of Acre.

July

This barren site, adjacent to an aqueduct, became our camp. We were very bewildered with the situation and especially by the French capitulation. Now, our new mighty ally, Britain, started to take care of us. We were given food and shelter in the form of tents, which we were taught to erect. We could not, however, understand why British soldiers were guarding our camp and patrolling it at night. During the weeks that followed, our numbers increased with a constant daily influx of newcomers, including a few refugees. Our initial number of about 200, most of whom had arrived here a few days before we came from Beirut, soon increased and in three to four weeks there were about 250 of us, maybe more. Colonel Koreš became the Officer Commanding of this diverse gathering.

To impress the British with our behaviour, we were told a number of rules which we must adhere to, so that we would be taken seriously by our new allies. Our camp looked spotlessly clean – initially, the order of the day was to "collect stones". This did not exactly meet with the enthusiasm of those of us who were privates, as by then about 30 percent of our total number were officers. As we all wore civilian clothes we expected that every one of us would participate in the daily chores. This was not so and we considered ourselves labourers – wondering if the whole of Palestine would have to be cleared of stones.

For the first few weeks our morale was very low. Hardly any news reached us regarding our Army and Air Force in France. All kinds of rumours were circulating in our camp. Eventually, we heard that many of our compatriots had reached England, travelling by all sorts of boats and tankers, with many of them reaching England via North Africa. After about four or five weeks, our situation slowly improved. We were issued with army shoes, socks, shorts, shirts and tropical helmets. We were also given our first pay, ten *piasters* per week, about one shilling (5p). All this boosted our morale tremendously and we felt that "they" knew about us and cared. Now we were eagerly waiting to be given rifles and start our training, so that we could participate in the war in some way.

Now being in uniform, it was easy to see who was an officer, an NCO, a private or just a civilian volunteer. Our ages ranged from seventeen to sixty. This created a few problems during our training, especially during drill marches. We were all volunteers and everyone tried to do his best. We had a few problems with our drills, as our officers had not taken the climate into account. English was also taught to those who wanted to learn. My limited knowledge of English from the Commercial Academy in Bratislava now became quite useful and I was eager to learn more. I managed to borrow a dictionary and learn lots of new words, often sitting for hours under the aqueduct, saying the words out loud.

From the very beginning of our stay at Camp Assumeria quite a few of the men did not believe me when I told them that I was a civilian volunteer and had never been in the forces before. There were some twenty people in our camp whom I had actually assisted in

Budapest or on the border between Yugoslavia and Hungary at Virovitica, and had helped to reach safety in Zagreb. Many of the others whom I had helped had managed to get to France before capitulation. Some of the men even thought that I might be working for an intelligence service.

Our much-awaited improvements, especially getting weapons and training with them, did not materialise for some time. We were later to learn the reason why. Our newly formed government-in-exile, now in London, had not yet been internationally acknowledged.

While stationed in this camp we were never allowed to travel anywhere else in Palestine, I suppose because we were not trusted. There was, however, one exception. We were taken to see Acre – the old town, fortress, dungeons, etc. This visit was made possible thanks to an escort provided by the British Military Police. The temperature at this time of year was very high. Our activities, i.e. beautifying our camp, collecting stones, waste paper, etc, had to be pursued in the mornings until about 11.30 and then again after 3 in the afternoon. We had to keep out of the sun, especially during the middle of the day.

Our food rations were adequate, though quite different to what we had been used to in central Europe. Despite this, no one grumbled, as most of us had arrived here exhausted, after having been nearly starved in Hungarian jails. Now we felt safe! However, one thing that we had to get used to was tea! We were told it was good for us and anyway there was nothing else to drink. And we drank it – to everyone's horror – with milk! We were also issued with bromide pills every day. The medical tent at our camp was run by Captain Fürst, a Czech doctor. The change of climate and the heat brought on numerous new illnesses and discomforts. Most of us were knocked out for a few days at some stage.

The Syrian-Lebanon border had now been sealed off and no more escapees or refugees were able to come through. However, there were a few new arrivals at the camp, people who had managed to reach Palestine via other routes. Jewish refugees who had arrived in Palestine prior to our arrival were in no hurry to join us, although they were Czechoslovak nationals. Many of them had secured jobs locally with far better pay. The Czechoslovak Consulate was still functioning here in Palestine, with the Consul, Mr. J.M. Kadlec, waiting to be given full authority, which was dependent on the acknowledgment of the Czechoslovak Government-in-Exile in London by the western powers and others.

August
Early in August we were moved to a new military camp, a sort of transit camp, at Gedera about 45 km south-west of Jerusalem. British units, including the Yorkshire Dragoons, the Leicestershire Regiment, the Royal Scots Greys, the Yorkshire Hussars and the Queen's Own were stationed there awaiting further orders. The amenities were excellent – NAAFI, cinema, kitchens, proper water supplies, toilets, showers, electric lights, etc. Our morale soon bucked up.

We found the British soldiers to be very friendly and were impressed by their discipline, manners and behaviour. We watched them enviously. This was my chance to improve my English. However, this mostly took place in the NAAFI, when drinking beer. Even drinks were provided by our new friends, as our weekly pay was still miserably low. I was not alone in trying to follow their "real English", as they were using quite a few words that I could not find in the dictionary. Eventually, I found out what the f-word meant and was advised by my new friends not to use it when outside the camp.

We were now properly dressed; on the other hand, we felt useless without rifles. We lived in tents, mostly eight men to a tent, in which we made a trench about 40 cm deep (to provide some protection against sand storms) where we placed our trestle beds and straw-filled mattresses. To stop the bugs getting at me I soaked the wooden bed legs in paraffin. Jackals were a nuisance too, howling most of the night. We enjoyed the films in the camp cinema and during the weekends we were allowed to leave the camp for the day. Next door to our camp was an orange grove. Moreover, the owner had abandoned his fruit, much to our delight. I had never seen or eaten so many oranges in my life. He said we could eat as much as we liked from the trees, as long as we didn't break off any branches.

Towards the end of August we received more rifles. We were very jubilant. Disappointment soon spread, though, when we were told that there would be only <u>one</u> rifle per platoon according to the initial allocation. So our training began, stripping and assembling our single 1919 Enfield rifle, in earnest. A few weeks later, additional rifles were allocated to us, boosting our morale immensely. Our training went on satisfactorily and we were able to take over guard duties from the British units.

On our weekend visits to Tel Aviv, and sometimes to Jaffa, we soon got friendly with the Australian soldiers, who immediately became our best friends and guardians. The "Tommies" were their rivals. They seemed to have very carefree attitudes and behaviour, and we all greatly appreciated their generosity. Even high-ranking officers would offer us a lift to town. I was given the addresses of two sisters in Sydney and Melbourne who were in the forces, or about to join up. This was going to help me improve my English. I did, in fact, write to them and they responded very enthusiastically.

September
We learned that many of our compatriots had reached England and that quite a few of our pilots had joined the Royal Air Force. Our government was also negotiating with the Russians to allow Czechoslovaks who had retreated from Poland and had been interned in Russia, among them my brother Ludvík, to join us in the Middle East, and to allow those with flying qualifications to join our squadrons in the Royal Air Force in England. The Russian response was favourable and groups of sixty to eighty men regularly started to join us. A transport of about thirty men with flying qualifications left Gedera for England. Some of the former internees from Russia appeared to be rather reserved and seemed to have rather misguided political views. We called them *hvězdáři*, stargazers (because of their Russian stars). After being debriefed by the British and Czech authorities they were allowed to join our unit.

On 30th September all the British units left and we, the Czech unit, took over the military control of the whole camp.

October
On 16th October, we were visited by General Wavell, Lieutenant-General Neame and the Foreign Secretary, Anthony Eden. This boosted our confidence again and we hoped that they would make some use of us.

Our pay improved slightly and we could get a pass to leave the camp freely in the evenings and at weekends. We managed to pick up a few words of Arabic, as the local people used to wash our laundry. Occasionally, when in training or on a marching exercise, we went through Arab villages. We were astonished to see such poverty and dwellings comprising small mud huts. The Jewish villages were very much more acceptable to our way of thinking and our way of life. The fields around them were cultivated and generally in a very good state. Their water towers usually dominated their settlements.

On 18th October a large group of us went on an excursion by bus to Jerusalem. It was certainly a very memorable event, with so many biblical places to see. It was hard to fully comprehend the magnitude of the past: the Omar Mosque, the Wailing Wall, the Mount Olive Church, Damascus Gate and David's Gate.

In our camp all sorts of preparations were being made for the Czechoslovak Independence Day commemorations on 28th October. Tents and the areas around them were given extra care and attention. Each tent was competing for top marks to be awarded by the officers in charge of their unit. We were told that on the day many dignitaries were going to come to our camp, including the Head of the Military Mission in the Middle East, General Gak, who at that time was based in Jerusalem. We were also going to swear our solemn oath of allegiance. The day came and we were ready for the celebrations. First, the inspection by General Gak and the British Administrator of Palestine, Sir Harold McMichael, accompanied by Lieutenant-General Neame and Major-General McDonnel. Speeches followed, given by General Gak, Sir Harold McMichael and our Consul General in Jerusalem, Mr J.M. Kadler. We then took the Oath, with a resounding *My přisaháme*, We Swear. The military agreement between Great Britain and the Czechoslovak Government had been signed in London on 25th October.

Our units were gradually expanding and our force comprised some 380 officers, NCOs and privates. However, there were far too many officers, about forty or fifty, and consequently only a few of them were assigned to command the existing units. My company commander was Staff Captain Zástěra and my platoon commanders included Lt. Khol and Lt. Štěpán. There were, however, frequent changes in these assignments, so that the best officers could be found to take charge in these unusual circumstances. (In the spring of 1940, it was estimated that there were some eight thousand Czechoslovak citizens in Palestine, but most of them had a negative attitude towards our military organization.)

Whilst in Camp Gedera I discovered that my teeth had suddenly started to crumble, and the only remedy recommended by the camp doctor was to have them pulled out. The other alternative was to find a civilian dentist, which I did, and pay for the necessary treatment. The total bill was £35. Our weekly pay at that time was about £1. I managed to borrow the full amount from Lt. Hlubík, whom I had met previously in Zagreb, and it took me almost two years to repay him. I thus acquired six gold crowns in my mouth.

Our training and various other duties in camp were often heavy and physically demanding. The age difference, from seventeen to sixty, and bodies in all shapes and sizes were not the only problem. There were quite a few professional people - doctors, lawyers, judges, etc. many of whom were Jewish, and they now found themselves as privates in our Army and had to participate in any work they were ordered to do. This included digging trenches and dugouts for tents as well as collecting and removing stones. Eventually this problem was solved by the British authorities who transferred them to their own units according to their professional capacities, though this mostly applied to those who were doctors.

November
At long last, on 1st November, we became an official military unit. We were to be known as the Czechoslovak Infantry Battalion No. 11 – East, with Lt.Col. Klapálek as Officer Commanding, and Col. Koreš as the Officer Commanding of the Czechoslovak Training Depot – East.

This re-organization created new posts for some of the officers, but most of them were kept in a reserve unit, the Officers Platoon, comprising about forty men. They were also paid less than the other officers. Although our weekly pay improved, it was still very much less than that of the British or Australian soldiers. We continued our guard duties around the camp and had further training. Our units were still well below strength and the influx of men suddenly stopped, perhaps due to the war between Russia and Finland.

Towards the end of November our whole unit went to the Jaffa firing range for rifle shooting practice. I was very pleased with my results.

December

In early December our platoon went to Gaza on a one-day excursion and a few of us had to carry rifles. This was an Arab town and we were not taken by it.

We had become quite used to enjoying the luxuries at Gedera and wondered whether our future camps would have the same amenities. We were going to find out very soon, as there was a rumour that we might be going to the Western Desert. The British offensive had started at Sidi Barrani on 9th December and was going well.

On 11th December the order came to move to Jericho. Apparently we had to go through this hell to get used to the conditions that would meet us in the desert. The only difference was that the Jericho camp was nearly 400 m below sea level. Our advance party put up most of the tents. The camp was situated between the Dead Sea and the town of Jericho, next to a banana plantation. So it became just the plain desert and us - no more amenities or luxuries of the previous camp, and the heat was unbearable, often more than 40 °C. We were surrounded by the bare rocks of the Judea Mountains. The desert spread towards the River Jordan and the state of Jordan itself, and a few miles to the south was the Dead Sea with its huge salt beds.

There were lots of scorpions and tarantulas everywhere and we were told to stay alert. In the beginning we slept with candles burning all night. There were two cases of men being stung by these creatures and they resulted in long periods of hospital treatment. The camp water supply came from the Judea mountains and had to be filtered. We were exhausted after a week or two: the dramatic changes in temperature – over 40 °C during the day and almost freezing at night, the *khamsins* – hot and dusty winds, scorpions, tarantulas, insects and malaria. We had to cope with everything. There was only one doctor and the medical orderlies were stretched to their limits.

There were no wooden structures at all in our camp. A huge marquee served as our mess. And we were beginning to get used to tea, especially tea with milk, which had been a complete novelty to all of us. Tea drinking in Czechoslovakia was uncommon and it was then only drunk with rum or lemon. Drinking it with milk was unheard of. In the heat, we soon found out that tea prepared the English way was perhaps the best drink for us. Marmalade in A10 tins, two per trestle table, became a permanent feature in our dining area. Marmalade was also a novelty, as hardly any of us had seen it before. We could not quite understand why the fruit had not simply been made into jam!

We started to explore the areas around us and on these excursions some of us had to carry rifles for protection against the Arabs. We went to see Jericho, the Old Jericho Walls and ate lots of Jericho blood oranges. We went swimming in the Dead Sea a few times and experienced the sensation of floating completely unaided. There was an excursion to the River Jordan, to the location where Jesus was baptised. On another occasion, we climbed the Mount of Temptation which gave us marvellous views of Jericho, the Jericho Valley, the River Jordan, the Dead Sea, and eastwards views toward Transjordan. We also visited an ancient monastery in the Judean Mountains, approachable only on foot. On Christmas Eve, I went on an excursion to Jerusalem and Bethlehem. We had to put on our winter uniforms as both towns were so high up in the Judean Mountains, and we also had to take our rifles. Fortunately, we were able to leave them at a military post during our two-day visit. I had an incredible feeling and lots of thoughts went through my mind when visiting all these biblical places, especially Bethlehem and the place where Christ was born. I thought a lot about my parents and the rest of my family, wishing they were here with me to share it all.

Back in camp we carried on with our training and on a couple of occasions we took part in tactical training against the Royal Scots Greys, who simulated parachute drops. On other occasions we participated in manoeuvres against other British units in this dreadful terrain – and were credited with good results.

1941 January
I was temporarily transferred to look after the telephone exchange. Apparently my English was considered adequate for the purpose. A liaison officer with the rank of captain was now attached to our unit.

February
By 7th February the British Sidi Barrani Offensive had ended. It had been extremely successful, with over 125,000 Italian prisoners being taken. Our conditioning here for desert warfare was coming along satisfactorily although we were still not properly equipped for full-scale involvement on the front. However, the High Command soon found some use for the Czech Battalion and on 24th February we left

for Sidi Bishr, about 20 km east of Alexandria in Egypt, travelling via Jerusalem, Lydda, Gaza, El-Quantara and the Suez Canal. Sidi Bishr was only a temporary camp. Our neighbours comprised some British units and some Free French units. After a visit by the CO for the Western Desert, General O'Connor, our Battalion was given second line duties, mainly due to the size of our battalion, which was still very much under strength. We had all hoped to be sent on as front line soldiers. However, this was not to be – yet.

March
Our orders to move came on 18th March. We were going to Agami, a town on the coast about 20 km west of Alexandria. Our duties were to guard the POW camp, mostly Italians, some Germans in El-Dekheila, as well as its airport and the docks in Alexandria harbour. With a battalion strength of 430 men this was a very strenuous task and we had round-the-clock duties, very often with only short periods of rest. On a few occasions, I was all alone, armed only with a rifle, in charge of 2-300 Italian POWs, marching them to various places to build roads. I had to order them to fall in *per quinque*, in fives, so that they could be counted. They didn't seem to have been enthusiastic about fighting, but they were good at road building.

Guarding a POW camp was not exactly an easy matter. The Italian POWs were given too many privileges by the British and many of the rules were abused. We were not allowed to take measures to maintain any strict rules in and around these camps. Guard duty in the port of Alexandria, against saboteurs, had its dangers too. There were frequent air raids by the enemy and there was a lot of pilfering by the Arab workers.

April – May
More men came to join our units. They came from Russia, Iran and Egypt, and amongst them were fourteen Slovak monks from a school in Alexandria – Frères des Ecoles Chrètiennes. Our Battalion strength rose to 759. There were now 47 officers and 712 NCOs and privates.

During my stay in Agami I paid numerous visits to Alexandria. Some of the sights were especially interesting – the statues of Muhammad Ali and Ibrahim Pasha, and the Colon Pompé, etc. Many places were segregated, i.e. only accessible to the military or to civilians. This was the first time we met the signs "Out of bounds", and "Blackout", often both signs together. Their meanings were very puzzling, we couldn't quite figure out how to translate them. We eventually found out what they meant when the Military Police tactfully explained.

Together with a friend of mine, Sgt. Karel Šefl, I visited the King Farouk Gardens in one of the suburbs of Alexandria and for a *bakshish* of £1 the caretaker let us into King Farouk's summer residence. It was beautifully furnished, painted and carpeted, and used only occasionally during the summer months.

Amongst the newcomers who joined us was a very skilful artist who had come from Russia. He managed to copy Egyptian pound notes to such perfection that he was soon able to start mass production! He was a heavy drinker too, and that lead to his eventual downfall and a jail sentence.

In camp most of us lived in wooden beach huts about 100 m from the sea and we often went swimming. Sand and sand dunes were everywhere. My room mate was Jindřich Křeček-Jituš, an artist and painter, who became quite famous after the war.

Our Infantry Battalion was at last acknowledged as a fighting unit, suitable for front line duties, although all our weapons requirements had still not been fulfilled. However, after a visit by the CO of the British 23rd Brigade, Brigadier Alexander Galloway, and under whose command we now belonged, the shortages of weapons were soon rectified with the help of a new liaison officer, M.B. Rowton, who was attached to our Battalion. On 31st May we received our orders to move to Sidi Hanish, close to Mersa Matruh in the Western Desert. The 23rd Brigade consisted of the Durham Light Infantry, the Border Regiment and us, the Czechoslavak Infantry Battalion. Beyond Mersa Matruh was the front line – and Rommel.

June
In our area there were a number of provisional airfields, literally comprised of a few jerrycans and barrels, which were used to indicate the landing strips. We were dispersed over a wide area, to guard them and to take action against any possible enemy parachute units. These airfields were at El Qasaba, Maa-Ten Bagush, Fuka Main and Fuka Satellite. For quick movement, we were allocated a few Bren carriers and some anti-aircraft machine guns. There were frequent air raids by the enemy, especially on the Fuka Main airfield. There were no

casualties on our side. We were mostly quartered in dug-outs or bunkers, which we had to build ourselves. There was a lot of activity, troop movements, being so close to the front. We soon learned that General Wavell had started a limited push on Fort Capuzza. Our unit should have participated as well, but High Command changed the order at the last minute and on 24th June we quickly left for Syria with the 23rd Brigade, travelling via a transit camp at Tahak, close to the Suez Canal. Here we were fully equipped for the front line.

July
On this front we were part of the 6th British Division. Our first fighting losses were one dead, Jiří Haas, and badly wounded privates L. Šil, L. Mancuška and B. Ondrák. Privates Lipa and Wiesner were slightly injured. All this happened when the French Foreign Legion artillery bombarded our position at the Beehive, the name of our hilltop dugout.

Within a few days the French had withdrawn further north and our units were now close to Merdjayoun. Before this, our two platoons were involved in a shoot-out with the Foreign Legion at Shebaa. There were no casualties. On 12th July, the 'enemy' was offered an armistice. Shortly after, the whole of Syria and Lebanon were surrendered to the British Forces.

On 15th July all our units moved to Aammiq about 6 km from Kabb Elias, an area which was full of mosquitoes, causing malaria and other illnesses. On two occasions we were able to visit Beirut, where life went on merrily, regardless of the war!

Our government-in-exile, now based in London, was at last recognized by Great Britain and the Western Powers on 18th July and our position in the Middle East became much clearer. We now felt we were of some importance.

August
On 4th and 5th August we received orders to move to a camp at Idlib, travelling via Baalbeck, Homs and Hama. Before this, my company went east to Palmyra where we stayed for about 8 days to help oversee the enemy surrender. This is where we saw French mobile brothels, organized in caravans, for the first time! In Palmyra, about 60 km away, there were many ruins and ancient remains, and numerous

pillars erected to commemorate glories of the past. The desert stretched for hundreds of kilometres. And the heat was unbearable.

Our camp at Idlib was situated in the suburbs of the town – in an olive orchard. We were issued with mosquito nets and those on duty around the camp wore muslin face covers. Our 1st Company was moved to Aleppo, to guard the railways. The rest of the battalion was spread out north of the Syrian-Turkish border, close to the Euphrates. Duties included guarding the border and checking goods and people at the different crossing points. My stay in Aleppo was quite enjoyable. I made a few friends among the British and Australians and met them in the evenings for a chat and a drink. The so-called red-light district in Aleppo was very busy. Queues for these famous houses started to form early in the evening – a queue of 150 to 200 men was not unusual. Every so often batches of 10 to 15 men were admitted. By 10 p.m. all the NCO's and privates had to leave, because from 10.30 p.m. the houses were open for officers only!

Around 15th August, Otakar Machek and I were sent to Baalbek to an Australian unit to take part in a two-week course in anti-tank warfare. Our English by then was pretty good. We trained on anti-tank guns, 20 pounders. We both seem to have made a good impression and satisfactory progress and we were commended for our performance on the range using live ammunition on moving targets.

Our stay with the Aussies was most memorable. Their friendship and attitude towards us was unforgettable. The friendship among Australians – privates, NCOs and officers – was exemplary, at least in this unit. Both the food and accommodation were perfect and the mess just to our dreams! And there were unlimited supplies of Australian canned fruit, anytime you felt like some! From here, we also had the opportunity to explore the ancient temples and ruins of Baalbek.

We returned to Aleppo where our duties were not exactly exciting. We were itching to face the enemy somewhere on the front line. There was a rumour that we would all be going to England to join the Czech army, already established and much larger than our units here. We felt that rather useless, especially as so much was happening on the different fronts. These secondary duties, performed by most of our units as well as by some of the British and Australian units, may have been the reason behind some of the boisterous behaviour when they congregated in the evenings in Aleppo. There were many fights between the men and, as the British Military Police had problems dealing with the Czechs, our HQ had to provide their own MPs. This seemed to ease the tension somewhat and a few of the persistent drunken fighters were put in jail.

On 30th August, General Sir Claude Auchinleck, who had recently taken over command from General Wavell, came to Aleppo. All our units were on parade on this occasion. We were all wondering where and when we would get our moving orders. Syria, with its climate, mosquitoes, malaria and many other illnesses (during our 4-month stay in Syria, over 400 of our men contracted some sort of illness) was not exactly a place to stay for any length of time. However, this was war and even our small battalion had to fit in somewhere. There was no space on the ships going to England, so we had to make do with the next best.

September
On 20th September, 24 NCOs and privates deserted from our units stationed close to the Turkish and Iraqi borders. All of them had previously come from Russia to join us in the Middle East. They took a 3-ton lorry, petrol and food. Later we learned that they had wanted to join the Czech Forces in Russia to help out "Uncle Joe" Stalin. They had been stopped by the Russians and then handed over to the Czech Military Mission in Tehran and detained. (They were later brought to Egypt to our training base, where they were court marshalled and put in prison. A few weeks later, in late March 1942, they all asked our president, Edvard Beneš, to be pardoned and, after careful consideration, this was granted on 25th June 1942.)

October
By 14th October 1941, my twenty-second birthday, we had handed over our duties to the Australian forces. Our orders to move came and we travelled by train via Aleppo, Homs, Hama, Beirut and Haifa, to a transit camp at Ez-Zib, just outside Haifa.

In Ez-Zib the CO of the Middle East Czech Forces, General Gak, came to review the parade. After a short speech, we knew that we were going to Tobruk. We were issued with new warmer clothing, battledresses, gas masks, etc, just as any British soldier would have been. On 16th October we continued via Lydda, Gaza, El-Quantara, Izmalia and Tanta to El-Amiriya, about 30 km southwest of Alexandria.

On 21st October, early in the morning, in the blackout, we reached the harbour in Alexandria and 624 men boarded two destroyers – HMS Napier and HMS Healthy. Another destroyer, HMS Decoy, was going to accompany us, carrying British soldiers. We all stayed on deck with our rifles and ammunition. After a few uneventful hours we suddenly reached the open sea. Our comfortable positions - at least that was what we had thought they were - were soon drenched with water. We were all seasick in no time, and after a few hours it was a question of managing to hold onto the railing around the destroyer. Huge waves frequently broke over the decks, and some ammunition and rifles were lost. All of us thought that this was the end, especially when we heard the U-boat alarm. This voyage certainly cured the ambitions of any of us who had wanted to serve in the navy. Even members of the crew became seasick and were as pale as death. As one of them put it, "Someone's got to feed the fish". We all wondered how on earth they were going to survive. Was it their own choice to join the Royal Navy or was it some form of punishment?

Later the same day we arrived at Tobruk harbour. We disembarked around midnight, making our way in single file along a wobbly pontoon bridge, about 75cm wide. We had reached solid ground. We were all soaked and felt useless and powerless. At the same time, an air raid and bombardment was in progress – as if welcoming us. Flares were lighting up the whole harbour and it wasn't until early in the morning that we reached a temporary destination. Within a few days we had relieved the Australians of their duties on the Tobruk Perimeter, the Red Line. Our platoon was housed in bunker no. 19, close to the Derna Road. It was an artificial cave under a huge rock, with a deep wadi in front of us reaching into no-man's-land. Defences around Tobruk were dispersed around its perimeter, with Polish and British units about 700 to 800 m from each other.

During the day our movements were limited, as we were only a few hundred metres away from the enemy. Even during the fifteen metre dash to the toilet there was a risk of being shot at. However, life on the front line started at night: first our meal was brought to us in the darkness and then we had to go on guard duty around and between the neighbouring bunkers, frequently probing into no-man's-land to detect and report on enemy intentions. With this sort of life, no wonder the enemy called us "Rats of Tobruk". The artillery and mortar bombardments of our positions made our duties at night extremely dangerous. Sometimes they only lasted for 10 or 15 minutes, at other times for 1 or 2 hours. It was impossible to move under such conditions, we just had to lie down and take cover. There were mine-fields everywhere, and only limited routes along which ammunition or food could be brought or the wounded taken to a field hospital. As it happened, the first injuries to our battalion were caused by mines, because the precise locations of the mine-fields were unknown.

To gain even more information about our enemy, it was necessary to stay behind in no-man's-land during the day, hidden behind a few rocks in the open. This was a job for two men only. Later, some wooden observation towers were erected around the Tobruk Perimeter, almost in no-man's-land. These were continuously bombarded by artillery and, on a few occasions, they were actually manned by dummies. Concentrated shooting and bombardment by the enemy was so intense that even the bravest person had to give up the idea of staying in a tower all day.

Our food was very plain – "bully beef" (corned beef) and "dog biscuits" (dry bread) and some canned vegetables. Water was in very short supply and tasted of salt. Occasionally we were given an allocation of navy rum. I found this undrinkable and gave it to the older men. This monotonous diet brought on many health disorders, and a few of the older men had to go to the field hospital. One night, torrential rain completely flooded some of our bunkers. This meant that everyone and everything had to be brought out to dry. Of course, the same thing had happened to the enemy and for a couple of days there was no shooting from either side, only the occasional wave as a sort of helpless gesture.

November

On one afternoon, to assess the strength and reaction of the enemy, our platoon and another platoon were sent out to try and get as close as possible to an enemy bunker and fire at them at close range. We managed to do this, though when we were within 150 m or so from them we heard orders being given, as our presence had been discovered. We had been able to get so close thanks to the advantage offered by the terrain on our side and the sleepiness of the enemy. However, within 20 minutes all hell broke loose and enemy mortar fire and artillery gave us some anxious moments during our withdrawal. Our encounter had been observed by the Tobruk CO and other generals and, at the most crucial moment, the Polish artillery, on Lt.Col. Klapálek's orders, came to our assistance with a barrage and enabled us to retreat without causing a major disaster.

We were told that it had been a very successful manoeuvre and we were commended for the achievement. Only a few men were injured. A few days later, early in the morning, at about five o'clock, the enemy opened fire on us with a terrific mortar and artillery attack on our positions. This lasted for 2 or 3 hours (after which time you just don't care about anything!). We were pinned down, wondering whether the enemy had decided to overrun our bunker. We were lucky, they didn't.

In the second half of November, we learned that the British Eighth Army had started an offensive and that we were soon to be liberated from Tobruk. Within a few days we could hear the sound of the artillery close to the town. Heavy tank battles were reported at Sidi Rezegh, a few miles from our position. We were continually on the alert, with orders to pursue the enemy on a given signal. Almost 14 days of critical battles were fought around Tobruk, with mixed success on both sides.

December
On 10th December we were in hot pursuit of the enemy. After a few kilometres our platoon was ordered to take up a new position close to the sea, as a precaution against air and sea landings. Some of our Czech units remained in pursuit of the enemy as far as Derna and beyond. However, they were soon withdrawn, as they were not sufficiently motorized and equipped.

1942 January – March
We were allocated new duties: guarding the harbour and the airfields near Sidi Rezegh and El Adem, guarding food depots and assisting in the transportation of POWs. Our hardest task was to guard and protect the food stores. Food was loosely stored in cases in the open desert at about 10 metre intervals over a huge area. On a few occasions, armed soldiers in trucks came to raid the stores and our job was to prevent them from stealing anything. By the end of March, most of our units were again performing duties close to Tobruk and its perimeter.

April – May
After handing over most of our equipment to the South African units, we left Tobruk for Palestine on 7th April, travelling by road via Bardia, Sollum, Marsa Matruh, Elo-Amariyia, Ismalia, Gaza, Lydda and Haifa. On 13th April we reached our destination – the Peninsula Barracks at Bath Galim, close to Haifa. Many rumours had been circulating about the status of our unit and we were pleased to learn that at last we were going to be reorganized and would then be known as the 200th Czechoslovak Light Anti-aircraft Regiment – East.

However, before anything was finalized, we were going to enjoy some leave, due to us after almost six months in and around Tobruk. Now was the time to spend all our savings accumulated during all that time in desert. Our interests varied so much and, after such a long time in the desert, it was nice just to see ordinary civilians, women, everyday life in the towns, to be able to buy things, eat real food and drink fresh water. Many of the boys spent their leave, and money, in Palestine visiting Tel Aviv, Haifa and Jerusalem. Quite a few of us went to Alexandria and Cairo. I joined up with another ten enthusiasts for excursions to Cairo, Luxor and Aswan.

On 15th April we travelled to Cairo by train and stayed in a small hotel for a few days. The hotel belonged to a Czech family who had lived in Cairo for many years. Our guides took us to mosques, the zoo and the Chinese gardens. We then went on to see the Giza Pyramids and the Sphinx and have our photographs taken riding camels. I also managed to climb to the top of the Pyramid of Cheops. It took me 16 minutes and I won the race to the top. After the guided tour of Memphis and Sakara I was even more enthusiastic about seeing Luxor and Aswan.

The journey by train to Luxor was extremely uncomfortable. Sand seeped in through the carriage windows, it was hot and stuffy and the atmosphere was oven-like. The next day, after reaching our destination, we soon found out that the temperatures in these regions were even higher than we had anticipated and could reach up to 55 °C. Our excursions had to be limited to mornings and late afternoons. Our hotel was situated close to the banks of the Nile. I had a very large room, with mosquito nets shrouding my bed. It was difficult to doze off for any long period of time at night. The air was still and hot and there were lots of chameleons crawling about in the bedroom. Everyone kept their windows open and their lights on.

The climate conditions and all the new experiences created tension and tiredness, both physical and mental. However, it was all worth it. We managed to see the Valley of the Kings, Tutankhamun's grave, the temples in Karnak and Thebes, as well as Aswan and its ancient granite quarry sites where obelisks had been cut and sculptured. Our guide had wanted to show us another temple in Karnak but this would have delayed our return to the hotel until well after 11a.m. We were unanimous in our decision not to see it as we could not take the intense heat. Someone even said to the Egyptian guide that he could keep his old stones - we preferred snow!

Luxor seemed quite busy in the evening, with many attractions and performances for the soldiers, and the local guides were willing to arrange almost anything for our entertainment. After some bargaining, we all went to see a private performance given by a young belly-dancer, under the supervision of a not too strict mother. Someone even said that this was his best discovery in Luxor yet! Next, we travelled to Aswan to see the very impressive High Dam on the Nile and to look at Lord Kitchener's gardens. Photography, according to the notices and our guide, was prohibited. However, for a small *bakshis* the guide would turn a blind eye! We then reached the state when we could just not take in any more. There had been too many temples, graves and stones, and too much sand and heat. We were all ready to go back and face our own civilisation, and we took the train back to Cairo.

On the last day of my leave, while wandering through the very busy streets, and with some money still left in my pocket, I bought a gold ring and had my initials engraved on it. This was done while waiting at one of the many stands which dealt in gold. I had never seen anything like it before: veiled women buying and selling gold amulets so casually and freely.

Our greatest problem in Cairo was keeping the shoe-shine boys away from our boots. They would deliberately smudge your boots or shoes, so that they could clean them again for a few *piasters*. The red-light district was run under the supervision and control of the military, aided by their medical units; it was very busy indeed. In our leave group we had about six cameras and we were thus able to record the sights of this unforgettable experience. I had borrowed a camera from Lt. Hlubík (he didn't get it back until after the war). It was 3rd May and time to get back to our new camp in Palestine, at Bath Galim near Haifa.

On paper, our new Light Anti-aircraft Regiment had already been in existence for a few weeks. However, in reality, our tasks consisted mostly of guard duties, drill, inspection, etc, all of which we now disliked very much. Almost every evening I went into Haifa, to cinemas, cafés, etc. At the end of May, news reached us that *Reichsprotektor* Heydrich had been shot in Prague (he died of his wounds on 4th June).

June

Early in the month we were given four Bofors MK III "ack-ack" guns (from the phonetic alphabet used by signallers in WWI, in which A-A, short for anti-aircraft, was pronounced as ack-ack) and our training started in earnest. In just a few days we became quite proficient at handling these new weapons. However, delays in supplies of Bofors MK IIIs, to make up the full complement for our regiment, continued. All training had to be done in turns.

An appeal was made for volunteers to train to become dispatch riders and I put my name down. I had always wanted to ride a motorbike. After my very shaky demonstration of how not to ride a motorbike, as I had never driven one before, I was told that with a little coaching I might perhaps qualify. And so, after seven days' tuition, I became a dispatch rider with a 500cc Norton, armed with a colt and armband and assigned to our Regimental HQ. I was soon able to handle my Norton properly, without having caused serious injury to myself or anyone else. On many occasions, after duty, I borrowed the bike and drove into Haifa for my own recreation and to the annoyance of the residents. Others joined up with me and Haifa's streets became our racing track! We were eventually found out and our exploits stopped.

About this time, the British gave the Czechoslovak Government permission to recruit Czechoslovak nationals living in Palestine and elsewhere in the Middle East who, for reasons of their own, had not volunteered to join our unit before. There had also been restrictions regarding Jews joining up, as Arab officials had been against the idea. Our pay was only £1 per week and as civilians they had been able to earn much more. Despite this some 600 Jews between the ages of 20 and 60 were recruited and our Czechoslovak Military Unit in the Middle East almost doubled in size to about 1,300 officers and men.

Also in June, our Military Union published a request from the Czechoslovak Air Ministry in London for volunteers to join our squadrons in the Royal Air Force in England. The response to this appeal was overwhelming. I was one of the more than 400 who applied. At this particular time, morale in the whole unit was rather low. Our eagerness to participate on the front and fight the enemy was somewhat dulled by the very slow allocation of Bofors guns and this also prolonged our training. Nor did having to train all the new recruits help our morale. After completing my training on Bofors guns, I returned to our HQ as a dispatch rider.

On one occasion I led a convoy of military trucks all the way down to Gaza to collect ammunition. This trip was to become an unforgettable experience. Under the intense heat of the sun, my skin peeled off my face twice during the journey. I had to report for medical check ups for two or three days. My enthusiasm for riding fast on my Norton was now somewhat subdued, especially during the very hot periods at midday.

The British forces suffered quite a few setbacks in June. Tobruk, defended by South African forces, was lost to Rommel. The Germans were advancing and continually winning battles. However, they were stopped just in time at El-Alamein, only about 100 km west of Alexandria.

July – September
Our training on the ack-acks progressed satisfactorily and in July we moved to our new camp at Ez-Zib, close to Nahariya, north of Haifa, for live shooting practice out towards the sea, at a target towed by a tug. The results seemed to have satisfied everyone as part of our unit was sent to protect Beirut while the remainder of us stayed in Haifa to protect the harbour. Later in August I was transferred again to dispatch rider duties. By now I knew that I had passed my medical for joining our air force in England. The final selection was concluded in September and I was among the lucky ones. We were envied by almost everyone, especially by my friends who did not pass their medicals because of some hidden handicap such as colour-blindness, poor sight and poor hearing. Until then, they had been completely unaware of any disabilities.

October – December

On 21st October we arrived at Suez and boarded our ship, the SS Orduna, about 15,000 tons. I had never seen an ocean liner before and I thought that the Orduna was colossal. Many troops and some civilians were already aboard, some were ill and some were injured. We left Suez on the same day. Soon after leaving port lots of orders and instructions were given regarding safety, especially about what to do if we were torpedoed during our long voyage. The Red Sea was considered to be quite a safe area. On the first night we slept below deck, but the heat there was unbearable. This problem was soon solved as everyone was issued with a hammock, a novelty for all of us, and we were able to sleep on deck. It took us a few nights and quite a few bruises before we could enjoy a whole night's sleep.

The officers in charge of my group issued numerous orders regarding our daily duties. Most of them were overruled by the captain of the Orduna as being impracticable. We had to curtail our activities to certain areas only. Otherwise, we were kept occupied by PT exercises, look-out duties and, later on, by guard duties, English lessons and singing over the ship's broadcasting system.

Our first stop was Massawa in Eritrea. We took on board some two or three hundred black prisoners of war. They were put in the lowest part of the ship and we were detailed to guard them. The stench and air below was overpowering and our guard duties were changed so that we were relieved at one-hourly intervals. The prisoners were packed on the floor like sardines. The temperature did not seem to affect them and they appeared quite content. Our elevated guard positions were close to the air funnels, a vital choice and it made it possible for us to keep our composure. The prisoners were only dressed in their underpants; most of them cleaned their teeth by rubbing them with a twig or soft piece of wood. Our next stop was Aden and we anchored just outside the harbour. A few more people joined us and we took on some cargo, perhaps it was mail.

We soon rounded Cape Guardafui and were then in the Indian Ocean. The threat of German U-boats kept everyone on the alert and we were all rather nervous. Extra look-outs were on duty from now on and the drill to abandon ship was practised. We were soon to cross the Equator and the temperatures both during the day and at night were overwhelming. Activities on board were reduced to a minimum. Even the prisoners seemed to quieten down. There was hardly any movement anywhere. The sight of the shores of Africa brought cheers and everyone relaxed a bit. We were told that Mombasa in Kenya would be our next stop. On 6th November, after some delays, we slowly made our way into the harbour and docked, the prisoners were taken off and more passengers and cargo taken on.

We were given shore leave and went off to explore the sights of Mombasa. We soon discovered that there was nothing much to be seen in the town itself, so four of us hired a taxi and drove out of the town for a few miles to see the jungle. One of the local boys demonstrated how to climb up a palm tree to gather fruit. The tree was about twenty metres high and he was barefooted. He climbed it as quick as a monkey and we rewarded him with a small donation. I also saw how pineapples grew, on short stems just above the ground. We also went to see a typical native village and the primitive huts they lived in. It had to be seen to be believed! We just wondered how they managed to survive.

After two days in Mombasa we set out once again on our voyage southwards. Twice, while in the Indian Ocean, we saw two British warships and this cheered us up immensely. They escorted us for a few hours and then sailed on ahead, zigzagging all the time. We had hoped that they would escort us but this was obviously not their task. We acquired a daily routine on board and, without any prisoners to guard, life became quite tolerable. However, I would have preferred to have been somewhere on solid ground.

Our next overnight stop was at Diego Suarez in northern Madagascar. Rounding the island we then sailed on to the port of Tamatave. After only a few hours we left, heading towards the coast of South Africa. By now, the temperatures were more pleasant but the sea seemed to have become rougher. We were informed that our next stop would be Durban.

We were given a lot of information about segregation, local ways of life and many 'do's' and 'don'ts' before we reached Durban. We were told that our stop would last for a few days and during the day we would be allowed to disembark. For security reasons we were told not to discuss our destination, length of stay, departure, cargo, etc, with anybody. Soon after docking on the 19th November we were given shore leave. Hiring rickshaws, we went to the centre of the town. I liked Durban very much and was determined to see most of it. Together with some of my friends, I managed to travel to almost every part of the town using local public transport. And it was free of charge for us. People were extremely kind, polite and generous. In the cafés and restaurants we did not have to pay either. We were told that someone had already settled the bill! It appeared that we were the first Czechoslovak soldiers in South Africa and the locals had heard that we had been in Tobruk. Hence the star treatment!

Durban was the first place where I saw men and women playing bowls, on beautifully kept square green lawns. It certainly was a sight I would never forget. One day, we were taken a few kilometres out of Durban to see a spectacular display of native war dances by two or three different tribes. Their near nudity and the sight of bare-breasted women was certainly a revelation and complete surprise to all of us.

We left Durban quite suddenly, after only about three days, as if the secrecy of our departure had been vital for our survival. Initially, we were escorted by two destroyers. The passage to Cape Town was very rough and we were quite relieved on the second day of our voyage to see Table Mountain. It seemed hours before we were able to dock in the harbour. Before we were granted shore leave new instructions were given about the locals and which areas were prohibited. However, this did not stop us from exploring everywhere, even places which were out of bounds. Most of the boys could not speak any English and this, in fact, saved us from a few awkward situations when confronted by the local and military police. Cape Town was a very busy place, full of sailors of many different nationalities. Because of our short stop here, we were not able to meet many of the locals or see many of the sights. Our departure put us on a northerly course.

The captain issued further instructions regarding various duties on the ship and a very strict black-out was put in force. The sea seemed to have calmed down considerably, but the danger of enemy U-boats was there all the time. We carried on with our daily routines: PT, English lessons and some guard duty. In our spare time we played cards and sang on the open top deck. Soon we were asked to sing for everyone over the ship's broadcasting system. About twenty of us formed a choir and a capable conductor, Lt. Král, led us to the heights of success! Our singing was very much appreciated and everyone on the ship talked about it. The most popular song was "Roll out the Barrel", as everyone could join in. To our great surprise, we found out that nobody knew that it had been composed and written by the Czech composer Jaromír Vejvoda, originally as *Škoda lásky,* Wasted Love, and the tune was taken over and given a new lyric by the British.

With all these activities the days passed by fairly quickly and we were soon approaching the Equator again. Very elaborate arrangements were made for the Crossing of the Equator ceremony. On the strict orders of Neptune and his court, quite a few 'victims' were thrown fully dressed into a pool that had been specially prepared for the ceremony. It was all done in a spirit of good fun. For most of us this was an experience of a lifetime. However, one or two of the officers did not take it sportingly.

The temperatures in this region again made us terribly uncomfortable. Some of us slept in our hammocks. Those in any enclosed quarter came out during the night just to get some fresh air. By this time we had made quite a few friends among the British soldiers. However, our knowledge of English was still very poor and it was difficult at times to understand one another. Everybody seemed to have an accent and a different way of pronunciation, especially among the ordinary soldiers. When they were in a group chatting, the f-word was frequently used.

After quite a long voyage without seeing any land, we were finally told that we were going to reach Freetown in Sierra Leone the next day. However, we were not allowed to leave the boat as the local health hazards were too great. The weather was still and humid. The boat dropped anchor about 200 m from the quay. Natives came up to the ship in their small boats and begged for money and we threw some coins to them. If any of the coins fell into the sea they dived in to retrieve them. Late in the afternoon there was quite a big commotion by the stern railings. Some of the sailors had baited a very thick hook and caught a huge shark, about eight or nine feet long. However, while the crane was hoisting it up, the shark managed to release itself by straightening the hook. An unforgettable scene.

This was only a short stop-over. Some cargo was loaded and we were glad to say good-bye to this rather inhospitable place. A two- or three-day voyage brought us into the region between West Africa and the Canary Islands. We were told that we would be passing close to large convoys heading south. We felt a little more secure, as there were quite a few destroyers escorting them.

The ship slipped into Gibraltar one night just before Christmas. There was a full black-out everywhere, except on our portside, where we could see lots of lights. We later realised that these lights were in Spain. There were many cargo and naval vessels in the harbour, lots of coming and going. We wondered what sort of life people could lead on this rock and how well it was protected. However, our minds were taken off Gibraltar as we received yet another set of instructions and had to carry out guard duty on deck during our final but most dangerous stage of our voyage to England. Our Christmas Eve food was a slight improvement on the standard rations. This was our third Christmas away from home and we were all reminiscing about past celebrations and wondering whether the next one would be at our real homes.

Our convoy left Gibraltar during Christmas Eve night. We could now sense the seriousness and urgency of our duties. Apparently, our route took us well into the Atlantic to avoid being spotted by enemy aircraft stationed at French airfields. However, U-boats were a constant threat and we had two or three alarms but no sightings. The weather deteriorated rapidly. Heavy seas, rain and sleet kept everyone, except those on duty, well below deck, trying to keep warm. We certainly felt the change in climate. New orders to maintain discipline and safety were posted daily, adding to our anxiety. We wondered whether we would actually reach our destination. Sea fog on our last day at sea did not help to ease the tension. However, the captain's announcement that we were now in British waters, and close to land, suddenly changed everything. The tension disappeared and everyone was chatting and smiling as if we had been granted the freedom to do anything we pleased. We said good-bye to our British friends and started to pack our few belongings ready for disembarkation. Late in the afternoon we docked in Liverpool. It was New Year's Day 1943. The calm and orderly way in which disembarkation took place left a very deep impression on all of us.

Camp Gedera

A favourite pursuit

Our first rifles

Time for lunch

"By the left...!"

My tent, Gedera, 28th October 1940

76

Secretary of State for War Anthony Eden, General Wavell and General Neame, visiting Gedera on 16th October 1940

Outside my tent in Camp Jericho, 8th January 1941.

Camp Jericho.

A PERSONAL NOTE TO EVERY OFFICER, WARRANT OFFICER, NON COMMISSIONED OFFICER, AND MAN OF THE 6th DIVISION

Owing to the extremely dispersed conditions under which we have been fighting and living, you will realise that it has been impossible for me to visit and speak to all units of the division.

I am therefore writing to each one of you this personal note.

The 6th Division is now composed of British, Australian, Indian and Czech Troops.

This is an excellent mixture from the fighting point of view, and will I know, add to the great reputation and fine fighting tradition gained by the Division in the last war.

I must however remind you that besides fighting qualities there are others to be aimed at and achieved.

The most important of these is Good Discipline.

Without this foundation fighting efficiency must suffer in the end.

In the 6th Division there are four different kinds of discipline; namely those of the British Army, the Australian Army, the Indian Army and the Czech Army.

There are good points as well as bad in all the above, and I feel sure that if we cut out the bad points and model our 6th Division discipline on the good points we shall have achieved a discipline second to none.

By discipline I do not want you to imagine for one moment that I mean the sort of "Prussian discipline" we have seen so often mimicked and caricatured on the music hall stage.

The type of discipline I seek is based on :
    a) An intense desire to reach Maximum Fighting Efficiency in all its branches;
    b) Good Appearance ;
    c) Good Behaviour ;
and   d) Good Manners.

These are the characteristics I wish each one of you to aim at, and for which this Division must be renowned.

Although the fighting in the Lebanon and Syria has ceased there is still a very great deal to be done in the occupation of the country which will influence the war as a whole.

It may well be that we are called upon at some future date to prepare for a campaign against the common enemy.

It is essential therefore to win over to our side the good will and support of the people whose country we are now occupying.

This can best be done by setting an example of a high standard of discipline which will have a far reaching effect both on the Frenchmen we have just been fighting, and also on the civil population who are looking to us soldiers to set the standard for the future.

Any lapse from a high standard of discipline will be magnified by our enemies out of all proportion and those guilty of acts of bad discipline will merely be playing right into the enemy's hands.

Finally, the highest test of a unit is the behaviour of the men when they are away from the immediate control of their superior officers.

                                          J. F. EVETTS,
17th July, 1941   Major - General,
                                        Commander 6th Division

A Personal Note..., issued while camped at Aammiq on 17th July 1941 by Major-General J.F. Evetts, Commander 6th Division.

Tobruk

German tank

British tank

Molotov cocktails

German road signs

Italian anti-tank mines

British anti-tank mines

Abandoned Italian artillery

Anti-tank gun position

DAILY CHEAP TOURS
TO
LUXOR & ASSWAN

Specially arranged for members of H. M. Forces by:

M. A. GABRY No. 1 Dragoman of the
N. Z. FORCES CLUB

1st. day		Leave Cairo Station at 7. 50 p.m.
2nd. "		Arrive LUXOR at 6. 50 am. Transfer to Hotel. After breakfast visit the Great LUXOR Temple — Return to the Hotel about noon for Lunch
	aft.noon	By carriage, excursion to the famous Temple of KARNAK visiting the fine avenue of Sphinxs, the great Court with its gigantic Columns, wonderful Hypostyle Hall Obelisks of Queens Makers and Thurtmosis, Temples of Amon and Mot, the Sacred Lake. Return to Hotel for dinner.
3rd. "		After breakfast cross the Nile by sailing boat to the West bank of THEBES Proceed by motor-car to the Temple of Deir El-Medina, Tombs of the Kings (including Tomb of TUT-ANKH-AMON) Tombs of the Queens, Rameseum Colossi of Memnon, Medinet Habu and Deir-El-Bahari. A luncheon basket is provided
		Return to Hotel about 5. p.m. for dinner. Transfer to Station and leave Luxor at 7.30 p.m.
4th. "		Arrive CAIRO at 7.0 a.m.

ONE DAY
EXTENSION TO ASSWAN
1st., 2nd., & 3rd. days as above

4th. "	morning	After early breakfast transfer to Station. Leave LUXOR at 7.0 a.m. Arrive ASSWAN at 10.30 a.m. Transfer to Hotel.
	aft.noon	After lunch visit the Town and Bazaar, then by sailing boat to visit the Elephantine Island and Kitchener's Garden. Return to Hotel for dinner.
5th. "	morning	Visit the Granite Quarries and by sailing boat round the Island of Phila Visit the World famous Assuan Dam. Return to Hotel on time for lunch.
	aft.noon	Transfer to Station - Leave Assuan at 3.40 p.m. Luncheon baskets will be provided en route.
5th. "	morning	Arrive CAIRO at 7.00 a.m.

All arrangements and programmes are most satisfactory and prices are fixed to suit all pockets.

Full details & advice on this trip will be given absolutely free of charge on application to No. 1 Dragoman (Gabry) N. Z. Forces club.

Daily Cheap Tours to Luxor and Asswan

Riding camels - Kotlín, myself and Pakan

In Lance Corporal's uniform, Haifa, 1942

On top of the Pyramid of Cheops

Mombasa harbour, 6th November 1942

Chapter 5: England I

1943 January – April

After disembarking we were taken to the railway station and given refreshments and tea on the platform by women dressed in some kind of a uniform. What a pleasant experience it was for us. At first, no one dared to engage in conversation with them due to our poor English. However, we soon managed to overcome this handicap, with their encouragement and understanding. En route to our new destination lots of people at various places and stations waved to us. What a wonderful feeling it created. During our two and a half years in the Middle East nobody had bothered to wave to us, least of all the local Arab populations. Relieved, we at last arrived at our destination in South Wales.

The Czechoslovak Air Force Training Depot was located in St. Athan in the Vale of Glamorgan, South Wales. The Officer Commanding was Wing-Commander Josef Duda. We were all accommodated in Nissen huts; the rooms were warm and the linoleum floors were spotlessly polished. And we were going to sleep on metal-framed beds with white cotton sheets and woollen blankets. What unexpected luxuries!

The dining room was spotless and for the first time we could choose a meal from a menu. A few of us chose "Welsh Rarebit", wondering why the name of the dish had been misspelt. When we were served cheese on toast and asked why, we realised that the dish was not "Welsh Rabbit"!

Almost immediately we were kitted out with blue uniforms, blue shirts, ties, etc. as well as white belts and brass cleaning pads for our buttons. It was with some difficulty that we accepted and got used to cleaning and polishing our buttons. We felt that, having spent nearly two-and-a-half years battling in the Middle East, this was just a bit too much "bull". However we soon changed our minds, seeing that everybody else was complying, and submitted to this basic requirement in R.A.F. aircrew training, which we had so eagerly wanted to be part of. There were daily parades and personal inspections. The inspections of our barracks – beds, floors, toilets – soon became routine and our high standards were eventually acknowledged by the O.C.

We found our daily drill a bit of a bind. First, an English R.A.F. unit would show us how to march on the parade ground, which they could do to perfection, and then we were supposed to copy them. It took us a few weeks to get the hang of it and perfect our timing. At this stage, however, the most important thing was to learn English. Few of us could understand or speak English very well and we were given lessons every morning and afternoon. We had a few more medical examinations and were given new injections. The medical was very thorough and some of the boys failed and were transferred to ground duties. Flying Officer Kozelka took us marching through countryside near St. Athan – as an orientation exercise. Flight Sergeant Vilda Jakš, the famous Czech Boxer, helped us with our training, especially with drill on the parade around. He was an air gunner and was later shot down in his Liberator over the Bay of Biscay.

We were also issued with "Czechoslovakia" markings for our tunics and great coats, white flash inserts for our caps, which denoted that we were Air Crew Cadets (all of us were demoted to AC2s, also known as "AC Plonks"), and identity cards with photographs. R.A.F. pay books and our service numbers had been given to us soon after arrival. At pay parade, our names were called out so that we could collect our pay from the Paymaster. When it came to my turn, and after a few attempts at pronouncing my name, the Paymaster often decided to use my R.A.F. number only, remarking "this is an awkward one"! On top of our English lessons we were taught aircraft recognition with the aid of slides and films, basic navigation, technical expressions and the meanings of important words that we would come across in our training. We also had to take our Vow of Allegiance to the King and Country.

We enjoyed going to our local R.A.F. cinema and most probably saw every film that was shown. At the beginning of our stay we were encouraged to visit Sunday afternoon tea dances in the nearby village. We could not quite understand why girls were dancing together or the dances themselves – the conga, the military quickstep, etc. It did not really help to break the ice between the locals and us, and we were shy to start up a conversation with our limited knowledge of English. A few of us went to Barry, a nearby town, seeking more exciting entertainment and to get acquainted with WAAFS and WRENS and others. We really enjoyed ourselves and found new friendships everywhere. It was a marvellous feeling and very much appreciated, being so far away from home.

After further medical tests we were graded and selected for final training as pilots, navigators, air gunners and engineers. However, before our departure to various training centres we were visited by our Air-Vice-Marshal Karel Janoušek and an English Air-Vice-Marshal. They welcomed us and at the same time impressed on us the seriousness of the situation. They also wished us "happy landings" during our training and later on when we were to join our famous squadrons, to defeat the enemy so that we could return to our homeland. In honour of the Air-Vice-Marshal we gave a performance in the Officers' Mess, directed by our very capable teacher, Lt. Král. Dressed as Arabs, we sang Czech folk songs and gave a short play. The whole evening was a great success and very much appreciated by our guests. The weather by now was really bad – mist, fog, rain, sleet, winds – we wondered whether this was normal English winter weather.

Shortly afterwards, our orders came and on 22nd February our party of 27 men, selected to be trained as pilots, left for London and the Air Crew Receiving Centre at Abbey Lodge in Regent's Park. It was a sort of recreational centre where we had a few lessons, physical training and quite a few swimming tests. Swimming was not exactly one of my favourite sports. We had to swim five lengths but this was beyond my capabilities! There was great confusion while arranging this test and, thanks to our unpronounceable names, my name appeared amongst the top ten swimmers, although I had only managed to swim two lengths.

Travel on the Underground was quite an experience for us. At first, we were surprised at how many people used it, not only as a means of transport but also as an air-raid shelter, especially at night. They were mostly elderly people and children, sleeping on their suitcases.

In the evenings there was always something to do. We were given complimentary tickets to the theatres and shows and also danced at the Hammersmith Palace a few times. We even received invitations to a private club. We also visited the Czech Club a few times, where our singing and enthusiasm livened up everyone's spirits, especially those of the pilots and air crews who came to the club to spend their holidays or days off. We were rewarded with plenty of drinks, especially beer.

There were many bomb sites in London. Some of the shops and offices were boarded up but often had a "Business as usual" sign. We could see barrage balloons all over London and the occasional air-raid did not seem to bother us. On one occasion, at Abbey Lodge, in the early hours of the morning, the sirens announced an imminent raid. According to the standing instructions everyone had to leave the building and take cover in the shelter. However, the ten of us in our room decided to stay in bed. This was reported to the O.C. who explained the seriousness of the matter. Regardless of our Middle East experiences we must now obey orders and instructions and also set an example to the young English recruits who were also billeted here. As a result, our drills were intensified!

Around this time, I managed to get some news of my brother Jaroslav from a friend who worked in the Czech Ministry of Defence. However, I could not meet him as the Czech Brigade was "somewhere in England", nor could I get time off from my training. On 13th March 1943 we received our orders to proceed to Paignton in Devon.

We were accommodated in the Tembani Hotel which was situated about 100 m from the beach and about 500 m north of the centre of Paignton. From here we marched to a country club, located behind the Palladium cinema, for our lectures. The Country Club belonged to the Singer family. It was a very large mansion surrounded by an enormous park. All our lessons were in English and the subjects included the principles of flying, engines, air frames, navigation, armament and meteorology, as well as communication using Morse code, signal flags and semaphore. Aircraft recognition in the beginning was rather difficult, as it was hard to understand the meanings of all the special technical terms. However, from our notes and questions we were able to get explanations and translations from Flt.Lt. Karel Horák. He was a pilot in the Czech Squadron and as he spoke good English he was seconded to our course, though he was actually supposed to be resting between operational tours. These sessions usually took place during our free time in the evenings at the Tembani Hotel.

Numerous aids were available at the classes – a Merlin Engine, a Tiger Moth biplane, machine guns, etc. – and these were ably demonstrated to us by a Flight Lieutenant. We nicknamed him "Mr

Follow me?", an expression he frequently used in the hope that we had understood everything he was trying to teach us. Daily PT and other outdoor activities were taken by an enthusiastic instructor, Sergeant "Chang". Weather permitting, we used to run long distances through the park and neighbouring woodlands always shouting as loudly as possible. This was supposed to improve our breathing and expand our chests!

We also took up boxing and rugby, then a completely unknown game to us. However, after two or three practice games, rugby training had to be abandoned due to too many injuries. We disliked boxing, but Chang persevered and we had to get up and box, though often simulating the fight, to the great amusement of the onlookers. To our delight boxing was also abandoned.

Initially, our daily march at 8 a.m. in the morning from the Tembani Hotel to the Country Club with an English NCO in charge was leisurely and we sang all the way. However, within a week we were forbidden to sing, as there were too many complaints from residents that our singing was ruining their sleep! After this, we had to march much faster – 120 steps per minute, increasing gradually to 150 steps per minute. We did not exactly think kindly of the residents!

Squadron Leader Chalmers, who was in charge of our course, tried to impress on us the importance of the various duties of the airmen and cadets. He was very keen on drill. One day he instructed all the Czechs to watch a squad of 20 English cadets performing a variety of different movements on one single command, hoping we would improve our skills and undertake training to do the same. And then he asked us "How d'you like that?" He gave up, disappointed, when we replied "Not at all!"

At night we had a rota for fire-watching around the Tembani Hotel. We were also issued with a stick, in case parachutists landed! After our Middle East experience this was really hilarious. Occasionally we were shown films in the Palladium Cinema, mostly of Battle of Britain dog-fights and other films to help us in aircraft recognition. Some of the weekends were spent visiting nearby Torquay and Brixham, looking for entertainment or finding girlfriends so that we could improve our English.

Halfway through our three-month ITW (Initial Training Wing) course, fifteen of us were selected to finish the course in two months. We then became known as the Advanced Czechs. The group included

Karel Fialka, Ilja Hrušák, Zdeněk Kopecký, Ladislav Kováč, Oldřich Kylar, Zdeněk Lípa, Otakar Machek, Karel Macura, Sgt. Josef Příhoda, Miloš Šafránek, Bořivoj Šmíd, Karel Štěpánek, Cpl. Josef Vavřik, Boris Zeman and myself. All of us had come from the Middle East, except Vavřik and Přihoda, who were already serving with Czechoslovak squadrons and had joined our course to become pilots.

Tension increased as we tried to get through the syllabus. Flt.Lt. Horák spent long evenings with us, preparing us for our final exams. Our biggest problems were in understanding all the technical words and expressions, especially in the armament section. On the evening before our exams we all got together and passed on everything we knew to each other, to give us all the best chance of success. To everyone's delight, we all passed! It was a very good reason to celebrate and we certainly did. Apparently this was the first time ever that an ITW course had been successfully finished in only two months. Our English friends on our course were quite envious of our achievement. We, the Advanced Czechs, regarded them as great individuals and good friends, but they were very reluctant to share their knowledge with others. Perhaps they were just too young, being both ambitious and reserved at the same time. Our own intimate friendship was already mature, sealed by the experiences of fighting in the Middle East.

And we still could not understand why everybody started a conversation by talking about the weather: Nice day today, lovely day, glorious day, hope it will stay nice, etc.

May

On 16th May we arrived at No.3 EFTS (Elementary Flying Training School) Shellingford, near Oxford. This was a Grading Flying School and here we were to put into practice all our accumulated knowledge flying Tiger Moths. Everyone hoped to be sent on a solo flight. Our instructors were Flt.Sgt. Ondřej Špaček, Flt.Sgt. Ludvík Mazůrek and F.O. Raimund Půda, as well as a few English officers. We were each issued with a battle dress, a flying kit and a parachute. The instructors took pleasure in taking us up on our initiation flights, showing off their skills, especially in aerobatics, and watching us go pale and, in some cases, become very sick! There was quite a lot of laughter when someone had to clean his Tiger Moth after a bad experience.

Flights usually took about 30 minutes and their main purpose was to get us acquainted with the reactions of the plane in various situations and for us to perform smooth turns and approaches, as well as landings. In some cases it was found that although they had passed all the medical tests, some of the boys could simply not approach and level out properly at the correct speed before landing. Consequently their pilot's training had to be ended.

The instructors competed between themselves, trying to achieve the highest number of successful solo pupils under their instruction. There were many anxious moments, both for them and us, especially before sending us on our first solo flights. A maximum time of twelve hours of dual instruction was allocated for this part of the course. There were many kangaroo landings during our first solo flights and some of the boys had to make quite a few attempts to land before eventually succeeding. Not having made a successful solo flight at this stage did not prevent us from proceeding to the next training level in our course. I completed my first solo flight on 15th June in a Tiger Moth, T7187, after just over 10 hours of flying. In the end, most of the boys were successful. After each first solo flight there was a great celebration, tossing the soloist into the air a few times and enjoying further festivities in the evening. On our final flight here our instructor took us up to Oxford and towns in the surrounding countryside. We certainly enjoyed this bird's eye view of this lovely part of England.

We were accommodated in Nissen huts, close to the green patch of land which was our airfield. There were no villages nearby, only scattered farms. We used to stroll around in the surrounding country lanes. Sometimes farmers gave us eggs, and tried to talk to us and be friendly. However our conversational English was still rather limited to "thank you, good evening", etc. We just could not make conversation to suit these occasions. Most of the evenings we used to play *mariáš*, a Czech card game and, of course, a few of the boys visited the local pubs, though they were quite some distance from our base.

June – July
On 17th June we were posted to the Air Crew Despatch Centre, ACDC, at Heaton Park, Manchester. On our arrival we noticed quite a few bombed out spaces, especially in the centre of the town. The scars after the German air raids in 1940 had been reasonably tidied up and

everyone seemed to be carrying on with their work as if nothing had happened. During our brief stay we were billeted in private houses about fifteen or twenty minutes walk from the camp, with three or four of us in each house, depending on availability and the size of the house. My group of four stayed only five minutes walk away from the Half Way House Pub on Middleton Road, Crumpsall. We had to report every day and join in the parade, and wait for the latest information regarding our next posting. There were a few hundred cadets, mostly British but also Norwegian, Dutch, Belgian, French, and now Czech. Long lists of names and postings were read out daily. Nearly all the British cadets had their postings delayed, which was a great disappointment to them. This was the first sign that pilot training was reaching saturation point. Many cadets had to be retrained as glider pilots, navigators and wireless operators.

We and other aliens were sure that our training as pilots would carry on, as our squadrons were waiting for us to fill in the gaps in their ranks. The British airmen were very envious of our potential postings. Many of the British boys were sent to the R.A.F. camp at Padgate. (Initially, we thought that this was their posting for further training. Actually it was just another camp, situated near Warrington.) Within a couple of weeks we were given instructions about our passage to our final destination – Alberta in Canada. We were advised to use up our currency as our next pay would be in Canadian dollars. On 7th May, we were all promoted to the rank of L.A.C, Leading Air Cadet, on six shillings and sixpence per day.

We often managed to miss boring parades or disappear when marching on the way to the public baths, trying to find out more about the Manchester attractions. Our absence was reported to the O.C. and as punishment we had to clean the WAAF toilets for a week. By this time our posting had been delayed for unknown reasons.

We had begun to become rather fond of the better dance halls in the city, the Plaza and the Ritz. However, we could not visit them often as we were nearly always out of money. On one of my visits with my friends to the Plaza, I chose as my dancing partner a girl who was standing on her own on the other side of the dance floor. I said to my friends, "That one over there is my girl. Look what a lovely undercarriage she's got." When the band started to play again I smartly rushed to her side, asking her for the next dance. And then I danced and danced with her the whole evening.

The following Sunday she, Joan, invited me for Sunday lunch with her parents. I was told which tram to take and where to get off, at Grangethorpe Drive. To me this sounded quite unpronounceable, so Joan wrote the address and other instructions on a piece of paper for me. This was of great help when I showed it to the tram conductor, who told me when to get off. I managed to find my way to 41 North Avenue, Burnage Garden Village, Manchester 19. I was very impressed with the house and the garden; they even had their own telephone! I was welcomed by her parents in a very friendly way. Sunday lunch was then served. It was roast beef with all the trimmings, which I enjoyed so much, even having a second helping (how little I realised then that they had given me the whole of their meat ration for that week). My conversation with her parents must have been a bit strained due to my limited knowledge of English. I did appreciate their kindly deed, feeding me and looking after me in such a charitable way. Mr. and Mrs. Bitton, Horace and Helen (Nellie), told me that lots of American soldiers had been billeted in the neighbourhood. Their presence was even more noticeable in the town, especially in the Ritz and Plaza. My friends were quite envious of my visit to Joan's parents' house and wanted to know everything about it.

A day or two later I met Joan again at the Plaza. I had to admit to her that I didn't have any money and could not arrange to meet her again; I didn't even have the money for the bus fare back to my billet. I promised to repay her any money she could let me borrow and she immediately agreed to lend me 10 shillings (50p). This enabled me to meet her in town a few more times. I was also able to help my friends out with their visits to town, with their bus fares. However, we often walked from Manchester to where we were billeted, simply to save every penny for our next entrance ticket to the Plaza.

Joan worked at the National Provincial Bank in Spring Gardens, Manchester. I was able to meet her at the main entrance once or twice. I was also informed that she had to take part in fire watching at the bank. This meant that she had to sleep there with some of the other employees. There was still a risk of German air raids on Manchester, the town being such a huge industrial centre. Fire watching was carried out just in case any incendiary bombs hit the bank, though only sand and water were available if anything did happen.

I enjoyed Joan's company very much and considered her my girlfriend. Many thoughts ran through my mind, wondering if I would be able to see her again after my training in Canada. We discussed this possibility and promised to write to each other frequently. I reassured Joan that I would repay my debt of 10 shillings from Canada as soon as I was able, though I often wondered whether Joan really believed me! This was not just a brief encounter: it was deep and serious involvement, although I may not have conveyed this then with exactly the right words.

At last our posting was announced, and we prepared to be sent to our next destination. On 29th July we travelled to Scotland by train and on the same day we embarked on RMS Queen Elizabeth at Greenock. All travelling was done with the greatest secrecy, taking care not to divulge anything to anyone. Careless talk could put us at risk. We were allocated our cabins, which were luxurious and very spacious. Four bunks replaced the original beds. The remaining cabin facilities would have been quite acceptable to first class passengers. This was certainly something that won our admiration and was an eye-opener for all of us. I had never dreamed that I would one day travel in such a colossus – the largest liner in the world.

We were given information about our voyage and strict instructions about where to go and what to do in case of a U-boat attack. We slipped out of Greenock so smoothly that we did not realise our voyage had commenced. As soon as we reached the open sea and the Atlantic Ocean it was no longer the duty of the escort destroyers to protect this great ship, and aircraft from Coastal Command took over. They kept in touch with us, flying in our vicinity two or three times a day. As a precaution against the U-boats our ship changed its course every ten or fifteen minutes, zigzagging across the sea. The speed of the Queen Elizabeth, perhaps twenty or twenty-five knots, was her best defence against being attacked by U-boats.

There were thousands of soldiers and sailors on board; quite a few of them Americans. The meals were served in a very orderly way. Decks and spaces were allocated for this purpose according to a strict schedule. Most of the time, however, we were confined to our cabins, entertaining ourselves by playing cards. About halfway across the Atlantic, we noticed that the aircraft, which had been keeping an eye on us, were no longer present. They must have been at the limit of their flying range. We were now about two days out of Greenock. We also thought that our position, somewhere off Greenland, would be dangerous because of icebergs. However, the captain assured everyone that we were not likely to encounter any, as the ship's route would be well clear of them. On our third day in the Atlantic the weather deteriorated, with very low visibility. We were a bit worried, wondering whether there were any U-boats in the area. On the fourth day the weather improved and we again saw aircraft. We were even more reassured when a U.S. Coast Guard boat contacted us and acted as an escort. After spending nearly eight days on the ship, it was a great relief to us all when we sailed past the Statue of Liberty on the way into New York harbour.

With the help of three tugs, and after a considerable time manoeuvring in the harbour, the Queen Elizabeth docked on 6th August.

The Tembani Hotel in Paignton

Follow me!

AC2s

A practical demonstration

The Advanced Czechs

Exams

Flt.Sgt. Ondřej Špaček and
AC2 Holl, Shellingford

Preparing for a solo flight in
a Tiger Moth, Shellingford

My first solo flight on 15th June 1943 in T7187, Shellingford

Chapter 6: Canada

1943 August
The welcome given to this magnificent ship and its passengers had already started during our approach, with sirens being sounded by many of the ships in New York harbour. It was all very assuring and very moving. We had to wait for quite a long time before we could disembark. There was great activity on the quayside and we were all wondering why there was such a delay. Then, quite suddenly, a military band started to play the American National Anthem and about thirty wounded American soldiers were carried off on stretchers to waiting ambulances. We found this rather strange, as we were not aware that Americans had been involved in any fighting in Europe.

After we had disembarked our kitbags were taken to Grand Central Station, a very impressive building. We were then allowed four hours to explore New York. This was a breathtaking experience: all the skyscrapers, the traffic, the vast numbers of pedestrians. It was just difficult to take it all in. It was business as usual, with no restrictions on anything. We found the people there very friendly and were surprised at the number of black Americans. We returned in time to join the train which was going to take us to Canada. Our destination was the R.A.F. Personnel Depot (PD) at Moncton, New Brunswick. Here we were kitted out and paid our first wages in Canadian dollars. Now, at last, we met up with comrades of other nationalities – Dutch, Belgian, French – all of whom were going to be trained as pilots, just like us.

Our stay in Moncton was a short one. On 16th August we boarded a Canadian Pacific train, and were on our way to our final destination. It was a very long and luxurious train and we were looked after by black conductors. Our meals were served in the dining coaches and our sleeping facilities prepared for us by attendants, and we slept between cotton sheets! These were completely unexpected luxuries. The vast countryside en route changed all the time, from forests and lakes to wide open expanses, with only a few scattered dwellings.

This was a non-stop journey through Canada and to occupy ourselves we played card games and read the magazines and newspapers which had been given to us. My favourite card game was *mariáš*, which we would start playing during the day and finish at midnight.

For the first time in our lives we saw how the automatic collection of post took place at a number of strategic points along the line, while the train was still moving at a good speed. After two-and-a-half days of travel, we were told that the train would stop at Winnipeg for about four hours and we would be able to stretch our legs on the platform. To our great surprise, quite a number of Czechs who had emigrated to Canada at the beginning of the century, had come to the station to welcome us and bring us some refreshments. They were so pleased to meet us, being able to talk to someone who had come from 'the old country'. And I was already wondering whether I would be able to visit my uncle Fridrich Kratochvíl, who emigrated from Russia in 1928 and settled with his family in Outlook, Saskatchewan. I remembered his address from home, but no one in the welcoming party knew them.

The countryside west of Winnipeg became more and more monotonous and uninteresting. Here and there it looked like prairie and was quite scorched, and there were hardly any sizeable towns. Quite often the stations only comprised two or three buildings, but each stop always had a large grain elevator for storage purposes. Farmhouses were scattered and very far apart and we wondered about the lonely lives of the farmers.

After having travelled more than 4,000 km in three-and-a-half days, we were glad to reach Calgary, Alberta. This was already quite a big town and from here we were taken to our destination, No. 31 Elementary Flying Training School (EFTS) at R.A.F. Station De Winton, arriving on 21st August. We were all going to take part in Course No. 88. The camp was situated in the prairie about 40 km south of Calgary. We could see the Rocky Mountains very clearly and wondered whether we would be allowed to fly over them. The following day we were issued with our flying kit and parachutes, and got acquainted with the layout of the airfield. The O.C. stressed the seriousness of our training and the strict regulations to which we would have to adhere.

We soon found out that there were a few Czech instructors here too: Flt.Lt. Karel Vildomec, W.O. Josef Flekal (known as *dědek* – grandpa), Flt.Lt. Vilém Murcek and others, who were working here during their rest period after having completed their missions over Germany. Some of them, because of their age, were not allowed to fly any more as operational pilots and could no longer participate in the raids. The notice board soon informed us who our instructors were going to be and I was to be taught by W.O. Flekal. I only found out from pupils from the previous course, who had stayed on due to illness or accidents, how famous a flyer he was, even in Czechoslovakia before the war, and of his daring flights at this station prior to our arrival.

On 23rd August our training started. During our elementary training we were to fly the Cornell, a dual control monoplane with a fixed undercarriage. After my initial familiarisation with the layout of the cockpit, the instruments and the controls as well as other relevant details, I was taken up just to get the feel of the plane in straight and level flight. It was quite an exciting time for us and when off duty we compared our experiences and, of course, our instructors too. After a few flights with my instructor and a solo test by Flt.Lt. Vildomec I went on my first solo flight. It lasted about twenty minutes and was very successful. My instructor was also very pleased, especially with my aptitude for handling this type of plane. This allowed him to take me through the entire training schedule without much effort.

We found out that quite recently, before our arrival, W.O. Flekal had been allowed to give a performance of his flying skills over the airfield. It had turned out to be an aerobatic display from his pre-war days, and was masterfully executed. However, this was never permitted again by the station commander as it was thought that it might have a bad influence on the pupils. It was also extremely dangerous – knocking off the wind-markers and flying upside down over the airfield only a couple of metres above the ground. I understand that the O.C. reprimanded him for his somewhat excessive enthusiasm. In between my dual flights and training I made numerous solo flights, practising all I had learned.

During the week we were quite occupied with our intensive training schedules – flying and attending lessons in navigation, meteorology, armament, aircraft recognition, etc, and training on a Link Trainer, an early type of flight simulator. For recreation, we were able to visit a nearby farm and go horse riding. At weekends, Calgary was our destination for entertainment. We found the Canadians very friendly. Most of the able Canadians had joined the Forces and many of them were participating in the war in Europe. Families had to cope with life without their menfolk.

One day the postman brought a sackful of letters for a friend of mine, Karel Fialka. This created quite a stir. Apparently, Karel had been in touch with one of his friends who worked for the Bat'a Shoe Company in Canada and told him how he missed his home and how lonely it was out here. (Karel had trained with Bat'a in Zlín, Czechoslovakia, before the war.) His letter had been sent on to the editor of a Czech newspaper based in Toronto. The paper had a good circulation in Canada and the U.S.A. as there were a large number of Czech nationals living in both countries. The result was overwhelming, especially from women and girls who wanted to correspond with him and cheer him up. Many of them even enclosed a few dollars to make his life easier. There were about 150 letters in the first batch, though the number gradually decreased to about twenty or thirty a day. He could not possibly answer all this correspondence and wrote to his friend to write to the editor of the paper to thank everyone for their letters and apologise for him not being able to answer them all. He became known as the camp Casanova. Even the postman was happy when his deliveries to the camp went back to normal.

Around this time, one of our instructors brought us a message from some Czech settlers in Blairmore in the Rocky Mountains, inviting us to stay with them for a weekend. We jumped at the opportunity and told them that a group of us would be coming by train. Both De Winton and Blairmore, 70 km south of Calgary, were on the line to Vancouver. Our first party consisted of: Zdeněk Kopecký, Oldřich Kylar, Otakar Machek, Karel Macura, Boris Zeman and myself. We arrived in Blairmore soon after midnight. There were about a dozen huge cars waiting for us, everybody wanted to take us to visit them, even just for a few hours. A few of the settlers came just on the off chance that more of us had been able to come. This was all very moving and was a quite unforgettable occasion. After three-and-a-half years away from our homes, it was the first time we had encountered such a warm and homely reception. We were looked after most generously and certainly enjoyed their Czech home cooking. Their ice boxes were full of drinks, and there was even our favourite "eye opener" – *slivovice*. Originally these Czechs had come to Blairmore to work in the coal-mines. Some of them had since found other employment or opened their own businesses. We managed to revisit them three of four times, which was especially important to Karel and Oldřich, who had found girlfriends there. On behalf of all of us who managed to visit the Czech settlers in Blairmore, especially to Mr. and Mrs. Žák, Mr. and Mrs. Poříz, Mr. and Mrs. Křivský and all the others whose names I cannot recollect, I would like to offer them our deepest thanks for all their kindness and generosity.

I also managed to get in touch with my uncle Fridrich Kratochvíl (now known as Fred) and a nephew in Outlook, Saskatchewan, and was able to make arrangements to visit them at the end of our course, as we would then be due for 14 days leave.

On one or two occasions my instructor took me flying over the Rocky Mountains, hoping that we would be able to spot a bear. He claimed that on his previous flights there he had seen one. Quite often, at weekends, he would go off bear hunting. Flying over the Rockies was an orientation exercise; we were not allowed to fly over the area on solo flights. Our navigational flights usually took us to the Lethbridge and Edmonton area. These trips were not too challenging as all the field boundaries and most of the roads ran in north-south and east-west directions, making map reading quite easy.

I kept in touch with Joan in Manchester, always receiving answers to my letters. However, these letters were written only when Joan was on fire watch at the bank! To keep my promise to Joan, to repay the 10 shillings that I had borrowed, I sent her a few dollars and some nylon stockings. She was most pleased to receive them.

About half way through the course, it was decided who would train to become a fighter pilot and who would become a bomber pilot. To our great delight, the majority of our course, including myself, were to be trained as fighter pilots. Ilja Hrušák, Karel Fialka and a few others were chosen to be trained as bomber pilots.

September – October

In September we were given our first taste of night flying, just for a few hours in a dual-control plane. However, before we were able to go solo at night we had to show satisfactory performance in instrument flying in the Link Trainer for a total of at least 5 hours. I passed that test too.

Our training was coming to a close and all our flights, under dual control and solo, were recorded in our log books with assessments by the O.C. of the station. I had 51 hours 10 minutes of dual flying and 31 hours and 45 minutes of solo flying. My assessment was "Above Average Ability".

We said goodbye to our friends the bomber pilots, who were leaving to train on twin engine planes in Moose Jaw near Regina, Saskatchewan. Our posting was to Medicine Hat, Alberta. But first, we had 14 days leave. Most of my friends went to Blairmore to stay with the Czech settlers, our compatriots, who insisted that we were all invited! I made my own arrangements to visit my uncle Fridrich Kratochvíl and his wife Marie, and their family in Outlook, Saskatchewan. They had managed to leave Alexandrovka in 1928 and had settled in Canada with their children Josef and Marie. Both cousins were now married and had families of their own, as I found out on my arrival. It was certainly a great occasion for jubilation and celebration. I had to tell them all about our family back in Czechoslovakia and they told me all about their years farming in Canada which, at times, had been very depressing. One year, swarms of locusts had eaten up the entire crop. However, with the help of the Canadian government they had survived. Now there was a war on they had problems selling their grain, which was heaped up in the open, in a field, all through winter. To me, this way of storing precious grain was hard to understand, remembering how my father farmed in Czechoslovakia. There, each grain was valuable! Canadian surplus grain during the war could simply not be exported.

I spent all my leave with my cousin Josef (Joe) and his wife Sonia and their children Eva and Ronald. They lived on a lonely farm about two or three miles from Milden, Saskatchewan. Joe took me by car over a widespread area, visiting other Czech settlers and distant relations. I was proudly exhibited to all of them and was very well received. They were all farmers – food and drink were in abundance. I was taken to the nearby farm of Mr. and Mrs. Staněk who were very generous to me, treating me as their VIP guest. They did not have any children. Joe told me that they were very well off and owned a lot of land. I was also invited to another Czech farm, run by the Glubiš family, about three times. They had two daughters, Rose and Emily, around sixteen and eighteen years old. They were quite likeable girls but I didn't pay much attention to them as they were rather young.

Most of the farms were widely scattered about the countryside and had to produce their own electricity. They all had windmills, which were used for charging batteries and pumping up water from their wells. There was plenty of livestock – cattle, pigs and poultry – as well as agricultural machinery of every kind – tractors, combine harvesters, etc. This enabled them to manage alone, with the help of their own family members, when looking after their big farms. If help was needed, they could always rely on a neighbourly helping hand from the other Czech settlers. This most memorable reunion with my relations came to an end, and they invited me to visit them again at Christmas. On 31st October I left for No. 34 Service Flying Training School (SFTS) in Medicine Hat for further training.

November

Medicine Hat airfield was situated about 5 km south west of the town, with the River Saskatchewan about 1 km to the north. We were accommodated in Nissen huts, about thirty of us in each. All the fifteen Czechs were kept together in one hut, the other fifteen were Brits. We were now kitted out with winter clothing and caps with flaps to protect our ears! The O.C. gave a welcome speech to impress on us the seriousness of our training and the importance of adhering to the station's standing order regulations. P.O. James became my instructor. After my initial familiarization with a Harvard Trainer I was taken up on 3rd November for a short flight. The Harvard had a radial engine which was rather noisy but you could feel the power behind it. It was certainly an improvement on the Cornell, our previous trainer.

Soon after completing about seven hours of dual flying and passing my solo test exams I was allowed to fly solo in a Harvard for fifteen minutes on 10th November. The flight was very successful and met with the approval of my instructor. From now on, after some further instruction, I was able to practise on my own and move on in the course syllabus. Previous instrument flying on the Link Trainer was a great help when we eventually started night flying and flying in or through clouds. My biggest thrill was when I was allowed to practise in the low flying area, just a few feet above the ground. The feeling was sensational. My flying progressed satisfactorily. On one occasion, in December, P.O. James told me that he would take me on a cross-country flight somewhere. I was able to talk him into taking me to Outlook, where my cousin had his farm. He agreed, providing that I could work out the course to get there. I managed to get us there and over the farm he did a couple of loops. I saw my cousin in the yard waving to us. However, we could not linger too much as our cross-country flight would have been overdue. This flight became our little secret!

December

Visits from Medicine Hat to the Czech settlers in Blairmore became very rare. The train connections and the extra distance made it rather difficult. At Christmas, I was able to visit my cousin Joe Kratochvíl again and spend a lovely holiday with the whole family. Marie, Joe's sister, who was also married to a farmer, Joseph Yesnik, lived a further 600 km away and she also came to visit Joe's family. And, of course, to meet me. There was a lot of snow about, making it difficult to use their car. Their propeller-driven "snowmobile", on skids, was quite useful at times, but it was very noisy. Marie wanted to know all about the family in Czechoslovakia, about our way of life, etc. I had a feeling that her marriage was not a happy one. This was later confirmed by her brother Joe. Before leaving my carefree holidays, I was taken to the Glubiš's and the Staněk's, on neighbouring farms, to say goodbye. I also promised to visit Marie and her family one weekend before I left Medicine Hat for good. I said my last good-bye to Joe Kratochvíl and his family and thanked them for giving me VIP treatment. There were so many things I was supposed to convey to my parents, brothers and sisters on my return home to Czechoslovakia. Being so engrossed in my flying and having such an uncertain future, I wondered whether I would be able to relate anything by the time I returned home.

1944 January

Back at Medicine Hat my flying progressed steadily. The different flying instructors made notes about my ability. Now and then our winter flying was interrupted due to heavily snowbound runways, but they used to be cleared after a day or so. In the meantime, we were given theoretical lessons in the assembly hall. Over Christmas a few of my friends had managed to visit the Czech settlers in Blairmore. Karel and Oldřich had been especially eager to go as they had girlfriends there. The Christmas celebrations and the hospitality they enjoyed staying with the Czech families simply crowned everything they had ever experienced. So did my visits to my cousin.

Towards the end of January I was taken up in an Anson, a twin-engine plane, for a three-and-a-quarter hour cross-country night flight.

For one half of the flight I was the navigator and the other half the second pilot. I enjoyed the experience but I was glad that I had been chosen to be a fighter pilot. Although I found flying enjoyable, on 29th January, on my first solo cross-country flight in a Harvard Trainer, I became really frightened for the first time when the weather deteriorated on my final leg to the airfield. I wondered whether I was going to make it. Everywhere was fog-bound and normal map reading was out of question. I had to fly very low in order to see the contours of the land directly under my plane. I was thus able to navigate, sticking to the creek, which eventually brought me into the suburbs of Medicine Hat. By this time my fuel gauge was indicating that my tank was almost empty. The airfield was a few kilometres from the centre of Medicine Hat and I wondered whether I would find it before running out of fuel. I managed to set my course correctly and when I approached the familiar station buildings I went straight in for landing, disregarding that I was flying with the wind, as the red light on my fuel gauge had come on. Seconds after touching down, my engine stopped and I had to leave my plane on the runway. It turned out that the airfield had been closed for the last hour and I was the only one on a cross-country flight. The control tower had been unable to recall me and there were doubts on the ground about my making it back safely. I was very glad to prove them wrong!

At this stage in our course we were all flying solo. Only now and then did the instructors accompany us to check our progress. As our course was due to end in March, these checks were important for our final assessment.

February – March

One weekend in February, I took the train to visit my cousin Marie Yesnik. Just like all the farms in the area, theirs was situated rather remotely, far from any town or village. I had to walk quite a few kilometres before I reached it. It must have been mealtime when I entered the house and in the kitchen I found the whole family kneeling around the table saying a prayer. It took a good five minutes before Marie could welcome me and introduce me to her husband Joseph and their young son David. I thought that Joseph's reception was rather cold. In the afternoon I had a few moments to chat with Marie. All the others had gone to work around the farm and we didn't meet again until the evening meal. There was a strange atmosphere about everything during the whole of my visit. It was obvious that Joseph kept his family under very strict control and Marie was very unhappy. My visit had not helped either, as I found out later when Joseph wrote to me, saying that my visit had affected his wife and her behaviour had become contrary to his wishes. My cousin Joe knew about Marie's situation but was unable to help. Afterwards, I only heard fragments of news about them through Joe, as he very rarely visited them.

We were informed that the date of our Wings Day, our graduation ceremony, would be 24th March. This gave us time to invite our friends, the Czech settlers from Blairmore, and five or six of them were, in fact, able to attend. The presentations were held in a hanger. There were sixty of us in the "88 Course" – British, Czech, French, Dutch, Norwegian – who received our wings and sergeant's stripes[8] from the O.C, a Wing Commander, of the No. 34 SFTS Course. We were very proud indeed of our achievements and the congratulations from our Blairmore friends really boosted our ego.

The next day, a Saturday, eight of us, all Czechs, decided to go into Medicine Hat and celebrate our graduation properly. The party comprised Miloslav Kolínský, Zdeněk Kopecký, Ladislav Kováč, Oldrich Kylar, Otakar Machek, Karel Macura, Boris Zeman and myself. We knew that the customary graduation dance was going to be held at the station and that lots of civilians, and young ladies, from nearby towns would be there. Being a bit older and considering ourselves more mature than most of the other cadets on the course, we decided to celebrate by going to a dance in the town, where we could more freely have a drink or two.

The place we went to was packed. We had been drinking, singing and generally enjoying ourselves when the R.A.F. police arrived. It was getting on for eight o'clock and they were looking for a Czech whose name they could not pronounce, with orders from the O.C. to bring him back to the station to start the graduation ball dance. We were told that the number one pupil from the entire course always got

---

[8] Sergeants stripes were awarded automatically on receiving your wings so that if you were shot down and caught by the enemy you would not be sentenced to hard labour, as would be the case if you held a lower rank.

this privilege. And it transpired that the name they could not pronounce was mine, Kratochvíl!

Three of my friends decided to accompany me back to the station in the R.A.F. police car and Zdeněk Kopecký came along as well, just in case they had made a mistake with the name. In the hall, where the graduation dance was to be held, the O.C. confirmed that I was the number one pupil for the "88 Course" and that I would be starting the graduation ball, dancing with a local beauty from Medicine Hat. I had to ask the O.C. to postpone the dance for half-an-hour, as I had had too much to drink and I could hardly do the honours. This was granted. I sat down on a chair and Otakar Machek massaged my legs, in front of everyone, so that I would be able to perform. This was my only dance that evening and I was rather ashamed of my behaviour. I felt that I should have been forewarned that I was the number one pupil on the course and what would be required of me on such an important occasion. I also found out that it was usual for the top pupil to get his commission. However, the Czech Government in London were not willing to allow this in our case, because they feared that there might be some unrest in our squadrons because pilots who were completing their second or third tours were still NCO's. My total and final assessment for the whole course, as a pilot navigator, was Above Average. I sent letters to my relations and friends to say goodbye and to thank them for looking after me and my friends in such an unforgettable way.

Our next move involved a two-day train journey to No. 31 PD R.A.F. Moncton in New Brunswick. We passed the time playing cards and debating our participation in the war, now that we were almost ready to take part. We also wondered how our friends who had been selected as bomber pilots had succeeded in their training, as news about them very rarely reached us. Our stay in Moncton was quite a pleasant one. We were kitted out with clothing, battledresses and other items we would need on the voyage and later in England. Now and then we got into hectic discussions with the French pilots who were on the same course. They seemed to be very undecided in their political outlook and not all of them were in favour of de Gaulle. We blamed them for not honouring their treaty with us in 1938 and for not being prepared to stand up to Hitler with military force. This usually brought our discussions with them to an abrupt end. The Dutch pilots had a much more sensible attitude towards the various European problems.

However, the problem of Indonesia did worry them and they already knew that they were going to be posted there.

A few of us managed to visit Saint John, the nearest large town, for shopping, hoping to find some bargains. We were very disappointed, as everything seemed to cost at least a dollar and our next pay day would not be until after our arrival in England.

April

Every month throughout my stay in Canada I had kept in touch with Joan in Manchester. Now that the time for my return was nearing, I wondered whether all those words we had written to each other had had some true meaning and had been expressed seriously. I wrote my last letter from Canada, informing Joan that I had won my wings and that I would shortly be coming back to England. At least the date of the voyage had been set and we boarded R.M.S. Empress of Scotland in Montreal, together with thousands of Americans, on 11th April. Most of the American soldiers were young and their behaviour did seem rather childish and undisciplined. We noticed that there were also many black American troops.

With the British and Czech contingents being in such a tiny minority, the Americans took over the running of the ship and all the daily routines. Cooking for thousands of soldiers was out of question. Meals were provided at specified times in the form of K-rations, i.e. pre-packed food in cartons; even cigarettes were included. These were quite a novelty to us and were generally accepted. Most of this six day voyage was spent playing cards and discussing our hopes and futures. With so many thousands of soldiers on board, we always had a visible escort of destroyers and planes looking after us. Practice alarms were sounded daily, and we treated them with great apprehension. We were quite relieved when we heard that the Irish Coast was not far away. The planes stayed with us for much longer periods and this certainly boosted our morale. The next day we could actually see the Northern Irish and Scottish coasts. Disembarkation orders were issued and we arrived in Liverpool on 18th April.

WO Josef Flekal (known as dědek-grandpa) and some of the new arrivals at De Winton

LAC Zdeněk Kopecký, LAC Ilja Hrušák, Fl.Lt. Karel Vildomec, LAC Karel Fialka

The Cornell

Instructors Josef Kubák and Karel Vildomec: with pupils at De Winton

De Winton airfield

Visiting Blairmore: Otakar Machek, Karel Macura, Boris Zeman, Zdeněk Kopecký and myself (photo by Oldřich Kylar)

Flying over Medicine Hat and the Rockies

Medicine Hat: No. 34 Service Flying Training School (SFTS)

Uncle Fridrich Kratochvíl

The Harvard Trainer

Cousin Joe Kratochvíl

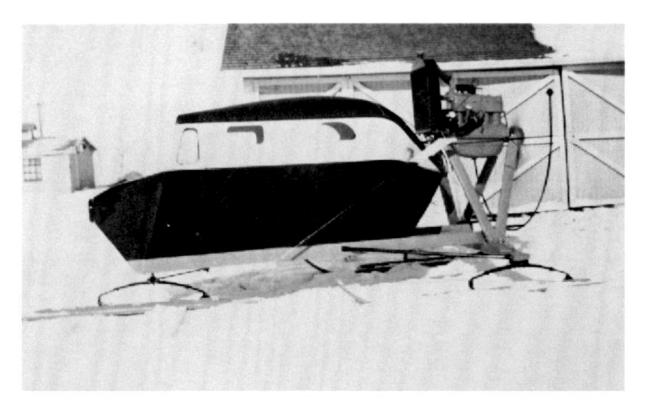

Uncle Fridrich's propeller-driven snow-mobile

Wings and stripes, 1944

Chapter 7: England II

1944 April – May
The approaches to the port were extremely busy with lots of other ships and tankers. Our disembarkation proceeded in a very swift and orderly manner. However, we could only take one kit-bag with us with essential items for daily use. Our remaining luggage was left behind, to be delivered to our new destination a few days later. We were marched off by a sergeant whose duty it was to take care of us. There were buses waiting to take us to the railway station, where refreshments had been prepared for us. Life everywhere appeared to be normal. Everybody seemed to know what to do! The blackout regulations hit us most. This certainly made us realise that the war was still on. What a difference from our carefree life in Canada! Still, we were glad to be back in England.

My brother Jaroslav was here somewhere; I hadn't seen him since leaving him at the Hungarian border on 26th December 1939. And I wanted to visit Joan in Manchester, wondering how things were going to develop between us! And, of course, I wanted most of all to finish my training and join one of our squadrons as soon as possible. After our experiences in Canada, the train journey to Harrogate was comparatively short. We did not have any idea why we were being taken there. It seemed to us that further training was being deliberately delayed yet we were told that our squadrons had a shortage of pilots. We were billeted in a large hotel near the Grand Pump Room, which had been taken over by the R.A.F. The Hotel Majestic had also been requisitioned and become the R.A.F. HQ. This is where we met daily to parade. There were hundreds of us, of many different nationalities, all of us air crew. The accommodation was excellent and so was the food. Our daily programme, carried out in groups, was read out on parade. It was mostly lectures about navigation, meteorology, etc. We also took part in clay pigeon shooting, swimming and PT. About one week after our arrival in Harrogate our other luggage came. We were very disheartened to find that many of our belongings had been stolen, especially our American cigarettes which were a highly valued commodity at that time. We reported this matter to the O.C. for investigation, but the culprits were never found.

News from the Russian front was very encouraging. The Germans were retreating everywhere. The Americans were here in England in great numbers and it was only a question of time before the second front would be opened by the Allies somewhere in Western Europe. However, our inactivity in Harrogate was quite demoralising. One weekend, about halfway through our stay here, we found a very nice pub on the outskirts of the town with very friendly service and customers. Someone even paid for a round of drinks for us. People were singing and generally there was a very cheerful atmosphere. On our next visit there, we decided to cheer the place up with our Czech songs. Everyone there was most appreciative and there were many encores! However, on the following weekend, when eight of us went to the pub again, and after having a couple of beers, we were asked not to sing again, although others were singing in the opposite corner. We were quite surprised at the change of attitude. The place was packed and when we went to replenish our glasses the landlord refused to serve us. This was the last straw for one of our flight sergeants, who had finished his operational tours in Wellingtons as an air gunner and had just been called up to serve as a fighter pilot. He approached the counter and asked the landlord to be served but the landlord categorically refused to serve any of us Czechs. This resulted in our friend picking up a soda siphon and smashing it against the display of drinks behind the bar. The whole display came down with a thunderous crash. We all left the pub, very dismayed about this sudden change of attitude towards us. At the next daily parade at the Majestic Hotel, we were singled out among all the Czechs, for our unruly behaviour, by the O.C. The matter was going to be reported to the Air Ministry, with the prospect of us having to pay for all the damage. We were astonished that nobody asked any of us why it happened. Fortunately, we never heard a word about the incident ever again.

  At last the news came through that we were going to be posted to No. 15 EFTS in Carlisle, to fly Tiger Moths. We arrived there on the 20th May. Every day we were taken by bus to the airfield, which was just a plain grass field. Our task here was to teach the new navigators how to map-read when flying at low altitudes. This was quite an enjoyable time, especially when we were practising in the Lake District. At weekends, we found Carlisle soulless and deserted. The only places open were church halls. The public houses were also closed. One Sunday afternoon, when we were looking for somewhere to go, we came across a notice board outside a building welcoming visitors to free afternoon tea and singing. We walked in, there were six of us, and after sitting down and assessing the place, we realised that this was just another church hall, and the people there were mostly women and children. Being the only servicemen present we felt rather embarrassed and soon, one by one, we departed. The area surrounding Carlisle was very flat and there seemed to be water everywhere. There were hardly any places to visit or explore. Then our posting came – to our disbelief it was Harrogate again!

June – August

On 6th June the invasion of Europe began in Normandy. The next day I flew on my last training flight at No.15 EFTS and from the 10th we were back in Harrogate. We were told that our posting this time would only be for a short while and we would soon be transferred to an AFU, Advanced Flying Unit. We went about our duties and enjoyed our free time, without any animosity from any quarters. At least we knew that we were going to participate in further training. Some of the British boys did not have this assurance, as there was already a great surplus of pilots. We were very pleased when our posting, to No. 5 AFU at Tern Hill, Shropshire, came through on 27th June.

The invasion forces had made good progress, although with some heavy losses also on the Allied side. There we were, not ready yet to be of any use. We flew and trained on the Miles Master advanced trainers with dual controls; they had a Bristol Mercury Engine, with quite a bit power in it. After the initial dual flying introduction and compulsory test, I was able to carry on training on my own, which was most enjoyable. A few of the instructors had already completed their operational service and among them were two Czechs. Their advice during training was invaluable to us with regard to our future duties.

We were billeted in Nissen huts, though this time we did not have to look after our accommodation. WAAFS had been allocated for this purpose. The sergeants' canteen was run on a very strict and professional basis. Daily parades were held as usual. It was summer and we were able to leave the camp and visit nearby pubs, especially at weekends when they used to be packed with servicemen and women. The general atmosphere was so much more relaxed. The hope that the war might end soon was in everyone's minds. I continued writing to Joan, wondering whether I would be able to visit her in

Manchester one weekend. In our free time, a few of us usually visited Market Drayton and sometimes even Shrewsbury and Whitchurch. Public transport from Shrewsbury, however, was very poor and I only used it once to get back to camp. At the airfield we had quite a few WAAF mechanics and they were very helpful when we had to check our magnetos by revving our engines. When doing this they had to lie on the tail plane to keep it down and on one occasion one of the pilots started to taxi towards the runway, with the WAAF still on his tailplane, pinned down by the airflow (and fear). The starter spotted her and saved her life!

The boundaries of our flying area were roughly Crewe – Stretton (also for emergency landing) – Chester – Ellesmere – Shrewsbury (also for emergency landing) – Telford – Market Drayton. Initially, we found that with this faster plane, the Miles Master, our map reading became top priority for improvement: there was no way that our skills gained in navigation in Canada could be compared to those required in England. Over here, you could encounter almost identical situations at road or railway junctions in any number of different places, making it difficult to determine your position. Compass flying proficiency, flying times, landmark recognition and listening to weather forecasts were vital factors if we were going to avoid getting lost!

Continuing on the Link Trainer, for instrument flying, was a very great help. Of course, our aircraft now were also equipped with an R/T (radio transmitter). Each of us had a call sign and this meant that we could get re-called if the weather suddenly deteriorated or, if we got lost in the area, we could ask the control tower for a course so that we could get back to base. This last option was only to be used in a real emergency! However, the R/T was only effective in our own flying area. We were soon introduced to D/N/F or Daytime Night Flying. We were issued with special goggles for this purpose and practised take-off and landing on a grassy area north of Shrewsbury, which was equipped with sodium lighting and a guiding system for landing. With the Miles Master having dual controls, our instructors were able to guide us and help us to land successfully. I managed to get used to it quite quickly and was able to complete a few landings on my own.

At the beginning of August, I was taken to a nearby hospital with a sore throat and declared unfit for flying for eight days. This was my first experience of a hospital. I was certainly well looked after! I returned to flying again, now mostly solo flights, with a proficiency check now and then by the Flight Commander. On a few occasions I encountered American planes with white stripes, the invasion markings, in our flying area. The pilots always wanted to start a mock dogfight. With my slower plane, and to their great annoyance, it was quite easy for me to get behind their tails, as I could fly in a much tighter circle.

One weekend I managed to visit Manchester and see Joan, staying at the YMCA. I wondered whether our relationship and friendship was still intact. Joan told me that she was going out with a Canadian and also with an American. I promised to come and see her again on my next leave, due at the end of my course and I received positive encouragement to do so. Our correspondence from now on became a little bit more frequent.

September
We now had Mark II Hurricanes, with Merlin engines, and they certainly had more power than the Miles Master. I soon got used to the plane and enjoyed flying it. However, I still had to fly the Miles Master, with dual controls, to complete my syllabus. We were also introduced to air gunnery, which we practised with a camera installed in the wing of the aircraft, aiming at a target towed behind another aircraft. At this stage of our training there were only two possible outcomes when assessed, proficient or not proficient. On our course, everyone was proficient!

The news from the Russian front was excellent, with the Russians managing to make great advances. The Allies on the Western front were meeting stiff German resistance, but making reasonable progress. The thought went through my mind – what would happen if the Germans capitulated before I could join our operational squadron? I was so eager to join and play my part.

October – December
At the beginning of October I went to London on leave, joining up with a few friends from our course. We managed to find accommodation near Paddington station. Most of the evenings we spent in the Czech Club, I think it was in Bedford Place, singing, drinking and generally enjoying ourselves. This was a place where many Czech air crews and others would congregate to enjoy Czech cooking and to meet fellow countrymen. And also to drown their

sorrows! For many of the Czechs in the armed forces, this had become their home, especially for those who did not speak enough English. About six of us from our course could liven up this club with our Czech songs in no time. This was usually appreciated with a crate of beer from one of the pilots who was spending his leave there.

It was here, on this visit, that I met Mrs. Ocelka again. She was there with an American officer: her husband, Wing-Commander Josef Ocelka, DFC, had died in an air crash in 1942. In 1940, when Mrs. Ocelka was escaping from the Germans, I escorted her from Bratislava to my parents' home. She had to stay with us for two or three days because of the deep snow. She was then taken over the border to Hungary by my brother-in-law Richard Koubek. She remembered this episode very well. Eventually, she had been able to join her husband. I realised that this was the wrong place and the wrong time to start reminiscing. I never saw her again.

Most of the last four days of my leave in London were spent in bed with a temperature. I was in agony with pain caused by an infected wisdom tooth. I went to the Czechoslovak Red Cross HQ to see what could be done – it was simple, they would just pull the tooth out. However, this was quite an ordeal and, in the end, the doctors had to chisel it out and plug the cavity. I was given some tablets to ease the pain but within an hour or two of reaching my accommodation I had to lie down, in extreme pain and with a fever. I could not eat anything and felt very sorry for myself and very lonely. My friends were enjoying themselves at the Czech Club and told me what a great time they were having. My plans, to go to Manchester and see Joan, had to be postponed and I wrote to her, promising a visit on my next leave. (We were issued with a Rail Warrant when on leave, which meant that we could travel anywhere we wanted at no cost.) About this time, I managed to pay a visit to Jaroslav while he was somewhere in the Midlands on manoeuvres. He was a tank driver with the Czech Armoured Unit.

At last we came to the final stage of our training, to be completed at No. 57 Operational Training Unit (OTU) R.A.F. at Eshott Airfield, where we arrived on 10th October. There were quite a few pilots of other nationalities here too. The camp was about six miles north of Morpeth in Northumberland. Nearby was a camp for WAAFS and there was also a canteen where we socialised in the evenings. Initially, we started our training on Spitfire MK IIs but by the end of October these were replaced by Spitfire MK Vs with 1470 hp engines. Our training was advanced and would prepare us for conditions encountered at operational squadrons. We practised D/F (direction finder) homing, low flying in the Lake District, low flying over the sea, cloud flying, formation flying, pinpointing, aerobatics, gun aiming, shooting, dive bombing, night-flying and cross-country flying. And we continued to practice on Link Trainers. The weather conditions were not always ideal but our training could not be halted. On one occasion, on a high altitude flight to 40,000 feet, I experienced an unusual problem on my subsequent descent to 35,000 feet. I could not move the lever to reduce my revs and, consequently, my speed. After a short time I reported this to the control tower and was told to stand by for my flight commander's instructions. Quickly, the chief engineer and my flight commander tried to assess the problem. They finally decided that I would have to switch off the engine and land by gliding down onto the runway. In the meantime, all the other aircraft were told to keep away from the landing area. During my final effort to solve the problem, and reduce my revs and speed, I managed to push the lever to the emergency forward position, and then bring it back to the normal position. I felt quite relieved when I was able to make a normal landing. I was never told what might have caused the problem.

Joan wrote to me that she would be helping out at one of the National Provincial Bank branches at Morecambe for two or three weeks. I was delighted to hear this and was able to spend the weekend there, managing to get accommodation in the same boarding house as Joan. We managed to see a show and enjoyed each other's company very much. At least that is how I felt. From now on we wrote to each other more frequently, planning our next meeting in Manchester, to take place at Christmas or on New Year's Day.

At the camp there were various forms of entertainment and also evening trips to visit Newcastle upon Tyne or Morpeth to see shows or go to the cinema. Neither of the towns appealed to me. Perhaps the bad weather had something to do with it. There were only a very few people about on Sundays. Our training was intensified to prepare us for our future in the squadron. We now used live ammunition in our machine guns and cannons for our practice shooting and dive-bombing. This was mostly done on a range near the coast. Section flying and night flying was introduced towards the end of our course.

With Christmas approaching, I tried to make arrangements to visit Joan in Manchester. However, this was not suitable for Joan. Instead, a group of us went to Edinburgh for three days. We liked the city but found it rather strange that all the pubs were closed on Sundays, and that rather restricted our activities. The Scottish people were very kind to us, especially Dr. Boog-Watson and his family; he was a great friend of the Czechs. They were always very helpful when we enquired about anything. However, in my mind I was already in Manchester with Joan. I was seriously thinking of asking Joan if she would marry me, wondering what she would say and what her parents would think.

The flying part of the OTU course finished on 28th December and everyone was given a week's leave. I arranged to see Joan on New Year's Eve, staying with her parents. All my friends from our course went to London on leave on 29th December. As I did not want to be on my own in the camp, I joined them and spent two nights in London, mostly at the Czech Club, celebrating finishing our course and wondering when our posting would come. On the 31st December I travelled to Manchester and was welcomed at 41 North Avenue by Joan and her parents. In the evening there was a celebration in the local village hall, refreshments were provided and there was even dancing after midnight.

1945 January
Joan had to work at the bank until lunchtime on New Year's Day. I met her in town and we went to the cinema, and in the evening we went dancing. The following day, after very careful deliberation, I proposed and asked Joan to marry me. We were both 25 years old and I was deeply in love with her. I explained that I could not promise or guarantee anything about my future in Czechoslovakia or about my work or employment, except that there was a good chance that I would be able to stay in the Czech Air Force. However, at present, I could only promise to look after her to the best of my ability. The signs were quite promising. It looked as though the war would be over in a few months. Joan did not answer my proposal immediately, as there were other boyfriends to consider, American and Canadian, who may have had similar intentions.

The next day, Joan must have broken the news to her parents. They were certainly pleased and advised me to delay everything until the war was over and I knew something more about my future. I explained to Joan that I could not accept her parents' suggestion to wait, as she was old enough to make up her own mind now. As my leave ended on 4th January, I suggested that she should think about my proposal and let me know in writing within a fortnight. Only she could find an answer to the dilemma in which she found herself. It was very sad having to leave Joan without her answer – wondering if I'd hear from her again. My friends were not much help either, knowing that my intentions were really serious. On arriving back at the OTU in Eshott, I was told that a telegram with my posting had been sent to Joan's parents' address. (I was the only one to receive a posting that day.) We had a small party in the canteen and the next day I was on my way to R.A.F. North Weald just north of London, where the Czechoslovak 310 Squadron was stationed.

On my arrival there I was informed that the squadron had moved out the day before and was now at Bradwell Bay on the Essex coast. I was given accommodation and the next day, 7th January, caught the train to nearby Southminster. I found that all three Czech Squadrons, 310, 312 and 313, were all here at the same airfield. Wing-Commander Jaroslav Hlad'o was in charge of the wing. Squadron Leader Jiří Hartman was in charge of 310 Squadron. My immediate superior in A Flight was Flt.Lt. Karel Drbohlav and later on F.O. Adolf Fornůsek. Within a couple of days of arriving at Bradwell Bay, I wrote to Joan giving her my new address, hoping to hear from her soon.

We were accommodated in Nissen huts. I soon got acquainted with most of the pilots from 310 Squadron. There were many pilots in the squadron who were doing their third, and some even their fourth tour of operational flying, and had been highly decorated for their services. Promotion to the commissioned ranks was painfully slow. All the Czech fighter squadrons were supplied with Spitfire MK IXs with 1720 hp Rolls Royce Merlin engines and one could feel the extra power they had, compared with Spitfire MK Vs. It was delightful flying: at first, in January, we flew locally and practiced flying in formation. Battle formations required very strict discipline. We practised cloud flying and R/T procedures. And we still carried on with our Link Trainer 'flying'. Some of my friends had been posted to the other Czech fighter squadrons, 312 and 313, and this made it more difficult for us to meet, as our duties and various lectures often kept us apart.

About halfway through January, I received a letter from Joan accepting my proposal of marriage – and it was with her parents' blessing! It was a very jubilant moment for me. Our correspondence increased to an almost frantic rate. I also had to find out what steps I would have to take and what I would have to do before we could marry. First, I had to apply, via the O.C. of our squadron, for permission from the Czech Air Ministry, giving full details about Joan and her parents. In due course, permission was granted, including a full explanation of how Czechoslovak and international law would affect us. In the meantime, Joan and I decided that our formal engagement would take place on 17th February and we also started thinking about a wedding date.

The activities of the Czech squadrons were somewhat restricted in January, mostly due to bad weather and frequent dense fog in the area. While we were stationed at Bradwell Bay, the so-called FIDO fog dispersal method was in use, whereby open petrol-fired burners, lining both sides of the runway, were lit. The heat generated dispersed the fog. My first FIDO-aided landing was rather a frightening experience.

February
The Allies and the Russians were making good progress on all the fronts. Our squadrons were mostly assigned to give top cover, at about 35,000 feet, to bombers on raids on German industrial centres. My first assignment was on 7th February when the Czech fighter squadrons provided top cover to one hundred and fifty Lancaster bombers during the raid on Dortmund. Other fighter squadrons flew at staggered heights between us and the Lancasters. When on long-range sorties our Spitfires were equipped with 90-gallon tanks, attached under the fuselage. In case there were any dogfights, these would be jettisoned to enable us to have maximum manoeuvrability – one of the Spitfire's main advantages. On this occasion we had received no warnings of any enemy planes. However, we did see one German jet, but this did not interfere with our mission. Close to the target we encountered heavy enemy flak at all levels. It was frightening to see shells exploding close to my aircraft. In a situation like this, the whole

squadron would take evasive action by varying its altitude by about 200 feet to make it harder for the ack-ack aimer to find us.

Before setting out to escort the bombers, we were given our final instructions in the briefing room. Only the pilots who were actually taking part were allowed to attend. And only then would we learn what the target was and what the latest intelligence was about possible enemy countermeasures. We were also told where and when to rendezvous with the bombers and other fighter planes, the meteorological situation and forecast, and our course, how long the operation would take and the emergency procedures in case of engine trouble. During ops the R/T channel was for emergency use only. We were also informed what vector (course and speed) to use in case we got lost, so we could find our way back to base. Our Wing-Commander had the final word, stressing the importance of R/T silence and giving us the time for take-off and the order in which the squadrons would leave. Questions from flight commanders and pilots were allowed and were professionally dealt with.

Usually, after briefing, we were ready to take off at short notice. The final order had to come from the Operational HQ. Immediately after take-off we switched on the oxygen supply to our helmets. This was a very important life-saver because within minutes we could find ourselves in thick cloud where a concentrated effort would be required from everyone so that we could keep in close formation and stick with our leader. The danger of turbulence and icing-up in the clouds was quite unpredictable. When flying over the sea, towards the continent, we checked our guns by giving them a short burst. The next day our squadrons were assigned to give cover to 18 Lancasters with a specific target – Ijmuiden in Holland, not far from Harlem. The mission was accomplished and we all returned safely to base. The following week we flew to the Münster-Rhine area on a fighter sweep.

While stationed here I also remember a V-2 rocket hitting the runway, about 200 yards from the Spitfire that I was just going to test-fly. The explosion created an enormous crater.

In the middle of the month I was able to get three days' leave. First, I went to London to buy an engagement ring and then travelled to Manchester on Saturday 17th February. It was a lovely reunion. Our engagement next day was strictly a family affair. There were so many questions and things to do because we wanted to get married in early April. Horace Bitton, Joan's father, still wanted us to postpone the wedding because there was news from all fronts that Germany would not be able to defend itself much longer, and he also wondered what would happen to Joan if I were shot down. However, Joan's mother, Helen, was in favour of us proceeding with our intentions. We set our date to get married, Tuesday 3rd April, after taking into account that our banns would have to be read out in our respective churches on three successive Sundays before. This was our next task to deal with. Joan and I were very excited and happy with our arrangements for our wedding day. However, I could detect that her father was still apprehensive, and perhaps rightly, considering my far-away home country and my very uncertain future.

I returned to Bradwell Bay in a very happy frame of mind. Now I was able to tell Karel Macura that I would like him to be my best man, as we had casually discussed this matter some time before. About this time, returning from an operational flight to Germany, we had to land using FIDO. The fog was as thick as pea soup. It was an unforgettable experience. Everyone was glad that they did not have to face conditions like these too often. On 23rd February, after one of our training flights in fog and bad weather, Karel did not return to base. We hoped that he had managed to land at another airfield. However, there was no news of his whereabouts. Not even an R/T call or a Mayday signal. It was confirmed later that he most probably lost his life in the English Channel. We were all very shocked to hear this news. His body and plane were never found. Despite this tragic setback, I had to ask our intelligence officer, who was British, about the formalities concerning my forthcoming wedding and the banns. He promised to let me know how to proceed.

A few days later, on 27th February, all our fighter squadrons were relocated to R.A.F. Manston in Kent. We were pleased to leave Bradwell Bay, as it was rather remote for our liking, too far from London, and it had more than its share of bad weather and fog. Our accommodation while at Manston was in Westgate, in a seaside villa which was used by the R.A.F. for its pilots. It was certainly superior to our previous Nissen huts. About eight of us were billeted here and we had our own batman to look after us. Daily, WAAF drivers took us to the airfield for dispersal and then back again, and also at any other time when required. The airfield had a very large runway situated close to the sea. We felt so much nearer to the continent and home. By this time, the Western front had moved so far east that we could not safely operate from this station. Arrangements were made so that we could land in Belgium and, later on, in Holland for refuelling. This enabled us to give proper cover to the bombers on their way to their targets and during their return flights. While in Belgium we were accommodated in a chateau, which must have been requisitioned by the Allied Command. There was no sign of anybody living in it.

On top of this, I had to see to my banns! With the help of our intelligence officer I was able to arrange this necessary ritual in a local church not far from R.A.F. Manston, and just in time as we had already set the date for our wedding. My new best man was Otakar Machek, a very good friend of mine, who was serving with the Czechoslovak 313 Squadron.

Comfort during our stay at the Westgate villa was very much enhanced by our batman, who frequently travelled to London and brought back Czech specialities. These included *parky,* a small frankfurter type of sausage*,* and salami from Ruda Poledník, a Czech butcher. Often in the evenings, when off duty, we patronized the local pubs. They always seemed crowded and jolly. Joan had written to me about her preparations and her banns, which were being read at St. Margaret's Church, Burnage Lane, less than half-a-mile from the Burnage Garden Village where she lived. I was able to tell Joan about my new best man and also about another very good friend, Zdeněk Kopecký, who would accompany him on behalf of the squadron.

March

On 2nd March, we were assigned to escort 250 Lancaster bombers on a bombing raid over Cologne. On our way, we landed and refuelled at an airfield, B-65 Maldeghem, in Belgium. On the return flight, it was every pilot's duty to check his fuel before crossing the English Channel. The minimum requirement was 10 gallons on the fuel gauge. Anyone with less had to land for refuelling. I checked my tank and told my Flight Commander that I would have to land in Belgium to refuel. We had an R/T frequency for this purpose and I was informed of the nearest available airfield. However, the control tower there could not give me permission to land as a whole wing of other fighter aircraft were in the process of landing. I was advised to proceed north to another airfield (all of this conversation was heard by our Wing-Commander). The alternate airfield, B-67 Ursel, had only one runway and the control tower there informed me that they were experiencing

90-degree gusty side winds. They therefore advised me not to land. Not having much fuel left, I decided to land anyway. Just when I was about to complete my landing a gust of wind lifted up the tailplane of my Spitfire and its propeller bit into the ground. The next day I was able to rejoin my squadron, leaving the Spitfire for a check-up! I understand that my Flight Commander should have stayed with me, as this was an operational flight.

On another occasion we escorted 900 Lancasters assigned to bomb the U-boat pens on Heligoland. We had to fly over parts of enemy territory which were still strongly defended, especially by ack-ack. The mission was successfully completed. On our return flight, still over enemy territory and at 25,000 feet, I noticed that my oxygen gauge was indicating zero. I immediately informed my Flight Commander about the problem, by waggling my wings and pointing to my breathing mask. He understood and followed me to a safe height, 15,000 feet, but certainly not safe as far as the ack-ack was concerned. They were able to concentrate on us with even more vigour. This was a really close shave! We both landed at our base without any injuries.

One of the most spectacular sights I ever saw was when we gave top cover to 650 Lancaster and Halifax bombers when bombing Cologne. The weather was good and within minutes the whole town was covered in smoke and dust. There were no enemy fighters to deal with. However, the ack-ack did claim a few of our bombers.

Sometimes, when we landed in Belgium, the operational programme was postponed until the next day, either because of bad weather or for other reasons. We were then provided with transport to visit Ghent or Bruges. We soon found out what we could barter for in the shops, especially lingerie and wine, if we could bring the owners commodities such as soap, coffee and cigarettes. However, this did not grow into big business. Towards the end of March our activities were scaled down. We were mostly kept in readiness for instant take-off should it be required. I was sent up with another pilot on one scramble to investigate a bogey, an enemy aircraft. We were guided by the Ops HQ, with the assistance of radar. It was very cloudy and the radar information was able to bring us up close to the intruder. In the event it turned out to be one of our own Lancasters, a straggler returning from a bombing raid.

Around 10th March, I was informed by our O.C. and Intelligence Officer that I would be eligible for free honeymoon accommodation and full board for one week with the compliments of the Lord Nuffield scheme. From the list of available venues we chose the Castle Hotel in Conway, North Wales.

On 30th March, the Flight Commander and I escorted a Dakota with a VIP to Brussels. As their cruising speed was much lower than ours, we had to circle around them in order to provide protection. We were later thanked for our performance.

April

On 1st April I travelled to Manchester by train with my best man Otakar Machek and my other close friend, Zdeněk Kopecký. Their job was to look after me until the happy event! Excitement was mounting. Various preparations had to be made and I really needed some guidance regarding the etiquette required by the occasion. After all, I was in a different country and intended to take Joan away from them into the unknown! Joan explained everything to me and from our arrival we enjoyed hospitality that we could never have dreamed of. Two nights before the wedding we slept at Joan's cousin's house, just across the road – Aggie (Agnes) and Jack Holt's kindness was very much appreciated. Our stag party certainly was a very jolly one. We went to a local pub and many of the other customers, on finding out who we were and what the celebration was about, bought us drinks – and far more than we could consume. We felt very honoured by their gesture. My friends made sure that I would be able to walk home. However, I did require some assistance. Back at the Holts, we had one or two more drinks and some cheese with pickled onions, just the thing to get us back into shape. I wondered what Joan was doing and was really glad that she had not seen me in my rather sorry state.

After a good sleep and with the help of my two friends, I was ready to face the day and the big event, our wedding. This took place at 12.15 p.m. on 3rd April at St. Margaret's Church. Maisie Anderson was Joan's matron of honour. There were lots of people in the church and Joan looked lovely. I was very proud standing next to her on this solemn occasion, though hoping that the church ceremony would not last too long. With a little help from the minister, I managed to repeat the vows quite clearly. The signatures on our marriage certificate were then completed – and Joan Bitton became Joan Kratochvíl. Quite a few well-wishers lined the path on the way out of church, throwing confetti over us.

The reception was held in Burnage Garden Village Hall and although rationing was still very strict, the caterer managed to provide an appetizing meal for us and some forty guests. There were colourful place cards for seating and two empty chairs for my parents, Pavel and Marie, marked *In Absentia*. However, there were no family guests from my mother-in-law's side as her brothers and sisters were devout Roman Catholics and had declined our wedding invitation. There were a couple of speeches, one with a hint of the speaker's misgivings about the way of life in Czechoslovakia and our future there. However, my best man, Otakar Machek, replied to this very ably and convincingly, expressing that our way of life was and would be very similar to an English one. After numerous toasts and well-wishing, we left the gathering and hurried to catch the train to take us to our honeymoon destination, Conway Castle Hotel. Our stay in this well-appointed, centrally situated hotel was simply marvellous. We felt rather guilty at the beginning, drinking cherry brandies in our room in the evening and then wondering how to dispose of the empty bottles! This was the first time that I had seen this part of Wales and I was very impressed. It also reminded me of Slovakia. We managed to visit some nearby towns and places and enjoyed ourselves immensely. There were so many things to discuss and plans to be made for our future, yet we could only dream about them. However, there were indications that the war would end shortly. Our honeymoon came to an end and Joan went home to her parents and her job at the National Provincial Bank. I rejoined my squadron in Manston and registered my marital status with the Czechoslovak Air Ministry. I wondered whether Joan would be allowed to continue working at the bank: she might have become an alien by marrying me. Joan soon let me know that she was welcome to stay.

Back at the squadron, our operational flying duties became less intense. The tremendous pressure of the Allies and Russians on Germany indicated that Germany would have to capitulate or be destroyed completely. Their first flying bomb, the jet-powered V-1, known as the Doodlebug, which had been introduced earlier and aimed mainly at London, had devastated many parts of the capital and killed thousands of people. Hitler relied on even more success with the V-2, a long-range liquid-fuelled rocket, and believed that it would compel the Allies to sign a separate peace with Germany. Just in time, the Allies managed to bomb and destroy some of the launching sites of this lethal weapon. The shocking news about German concentration camps and atrocities were reaching us daily, especially from April onwards. The Americans made rapid progress in Southern Germany and the Russians were on the outskirts of Berlin. British forces made good gains in Northern Germany.

May

On 2nd May, the whole wing of the Czech squadrons was ordered to fly an operational mission to Germany. After only 10 minutes in the air, the mission was aborted, as it was learned that enemy forces in Northern Germany were on the verge of surrender. The Wing-Commander was given permission to carry out a practice flight in formation, involving the whole wing, to Exeter before returning to Manston.

The weather was bad with a very low cloud base. On our return flight over Surrey – the Haslemere area – my engine would not give any thrust. I switched over from the long-range fuel tank to the normal fuel supply, but no joy there either. Rapidly losing height and only fifty or sixty feet above the ground over wooded hills, I was lucky to spot a small potato field near a farm[9]. To get to it, I had to risk hitting a tree with one of the wings. Unfortunately, I did hit it and, with a rolling movement, crashed in the field, my Spitfire turning upside down. Momentarily, I was knocked out. I regained consciousness and although I had had my hood open before crashing I could not squeeze out from underneath the plane. I was completely pinned to the ground. Only my left arm and my head were sticking out of the cockpit. I could also smell something smouldering in the cockpit and then felt something burning on my battledress knee. Within minutes, about three or four men (the farmer and farmhands) came to my rescue. Not having any spades with them, they tried to pull me out from this dangerous position. I even overheard them saying not to pull so hard on my arm, as it might come off! I asked them to use their hands to move some soil from underneath me and then pull as hard as they could, as I was afraid the plane might blow up, with all the fuel and ammunition still on board. They finally succeeded in pulling me out

---

[9] I crashed on J. Humphrey's Upper Fold Farm, Fernhurst, Surrey.

and dragging me away from the plane. I understand the plane burnt up shortly after my rescue.

Not long after, two or three ambulances arrived, alerted by aircraft spotters, and took me to Oxbridge Hospital in London. Having some burns, the next day I was transferred to the Princess Mary's R.A.F. Hospital Halton, near Aylesbury for treatment. I was told that my wife had been informed and I was able to ring her and assure her that I was alright. Joan promised to visit me the following weekend and this cheered me up a lot. I was able to explain to her what had happened and what treatment I was getting. She was not quite happy with the explanations I gave her and asked me to urge the doctors to examine my neck (apparently I was holding my head sideways without realising it). I was sent to be X-rayed and the doctors discovered that I had dislocated my neck between the third and fourth vertebrae.

I had an unexpected visit when three pilots, F.O. Bedřich Fröhlich, Sgt. Bořivoj Šmíd and W.O. Jan Kravec, flew in to see me – and gave me the latest news about 310 Squadron, which was still at Manston. At that point, there was no news about the squadron flying home to Prague, though I knew then, because of my condition, that I would not be able to join them. The war in Europe had come to an end officially on 8th May.

The doctors decided to put me in plaster, which covered most of the upper part of my body, leaving free only my arms and face from my chin upwards. This meant I was able to see the sky and I could walk. I had problems with eating and drinking. The first few days in plaster were sheer torture. With the plaster drying out I felt like being refrigerated. I could only lie on my back. I could not turn over at all. I had to be assisted by nurses to take me to the loo. On about the fifth day the plaster had dried out. I was even able to sleep for a few hours. I was often given sleeping pills to help me sleep. My hospital bed had a special gadget with a chain above my bed, thus I was eventually able to lift myself up and get up from my bed. Joan came to see me again and suggested that I could perhaps come to Manchester and stay with her parents on my leave. The doctors agreed to this and a few days later I was given twenty-eight days sick leave.

As a married Flight Sergeant, my wages at this time were 14s.9d (74p) a day. Joan and I decided that we could save my wages while she was still working at the bank, so I stopped drawing them, hoping to have a lump sum on my discharge from hospital. I spent my sick leave at Joan's house. Her mother was a trained nurse and the attention I was given was really first class. By now my bones had almost healed though my plaster still felt rather uncomfortable. Joan was sometimes able to scratch the itching parts of my chest and back with knitting needles. I was always given preferential treatment whenever I travelled by bus or when queueing to see a film. In the cinema, I always sat in the second row with an empty seat in front of me, as I had to bend well forward in order to see the screen. Everybody was simply marvellous.

I heard no further news from 310 Squadron and wondered whether they had flown back to Czechoslovakia. The Czechoslovak Independent Armoured Brigade, which had fought in Dunkirk, arrived home in Czechoslovakia during the second half of May.

July

At the beginning of July, I went back to the hospital at R.A.F. Halton for further checks. The doctors decided to keep my plaster on for a few more weeks and I was given another three weeks' sick leave. I was glad to be able to rejoin Joan and enjoy her parents' hospitality. I wondered whether my brother Jaroslav had been able to visit our home and pass the message on to my parents that I was still alive. Joan received some preliminary information from the Czechoslovak authorities in London about her being on the list for repatriation. Although I felt very much better, I still felt quite useless.

At the end of July, I was re-admitted to R.A.F. Halton, hoping this time that I would be able to have my plaster removed. It took quite a few days before the doctors decided to do so. I had urged them to take it off, as I felt very uncomfortable and hoped to be discharged from the hospital immediately. How wrong I was, as it turned out, for when all the plaster was cut and removed two nurses standing by had to save me from collapsing. I was put on a bed and this time soft bandages were used to give me support. After a few days, I regained my strength and was able to move about freely. However, I still felt stiff in my neck. A few more X-rays gave assurance that my dislocation was on the mend and that I would be fit again. I was given another three weeks' sick leave, this time with convalescence in Cemaes Bay, Anglesey, North Wales.

August
Joan was able to come with me to Anglesey. We were able to dream about our future in a very quiet atmosphere. Long walks and evening visits to the local pub were the only things we could do. All this, however, helped to restore my health and allowed us to get to know each other better before having to return to hospital. Joan and I also managed to visit the Humphrey's Farm in Surrey to thank them for saving my life. Their generous hospitality was simply wonderful. Joan received further information and guidance regarding her repatriation to Czechoslovakia, although no definite date had yet been set. After three days in hospital at R.A.F. Halton, I had my final medical check and on 12th September I was classified A1B (fit for full flying duties and ground duties). That meant I could fly again! Orders came to proceed back to my unit for duty – to R.A.F. Manston. Delighted with the news about my health, I phoned Joan immediately. I felt on top of the world.

August – September
Arriving at R.A.F. Manston, I was given all my issued items – clothing, accessories, colt, etc, which had been stored there after my crash. I also intended to withdraw my accumulated pay from the paymaster and send it to Joan to purchase some items for our future home. The paymaster informed me that my savings had already been transferred to the Czech Air Ministry and would be paid to me in Czechoslovakia, in Czech currency. Needless to say, I felt somewhat cheated.

Ready for a flight in my Miles Master at No.5 AFU, Tern Hill

Flying in formation, Miles Masters, Tern Hill

No. 57 OTU at RAF Eshott

Marriage to Joan Eileen Bitton on 3rd April 1945

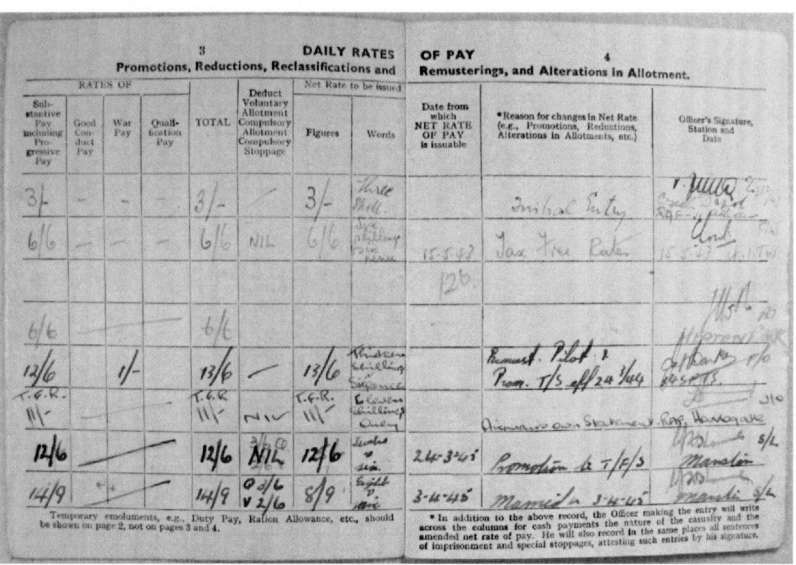

Pay book: new wages on promotion to Flight Sergeant and on becoming married

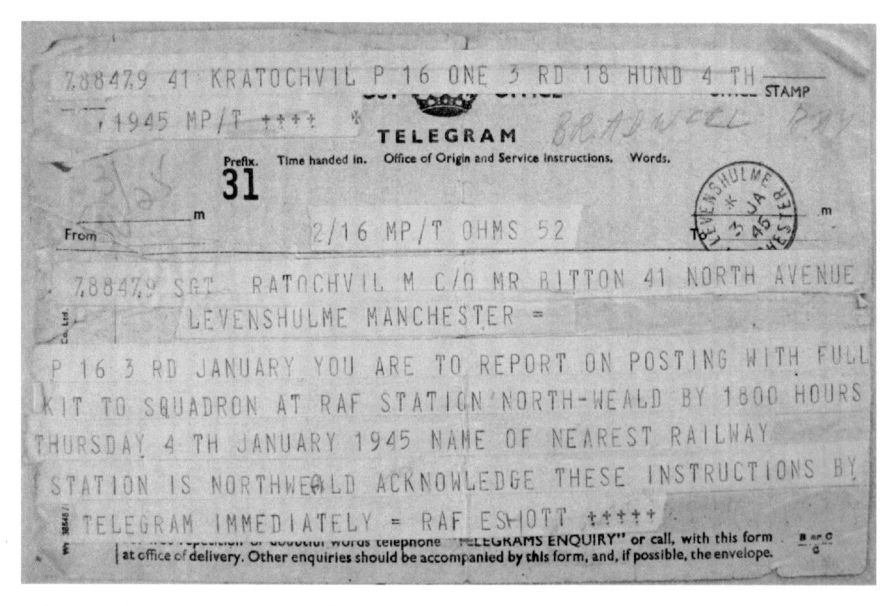

My posting to 310 Squadron

Spitfire Mark IX, Manston

Billets in Westgate on Sea, close to Margate

310 Squadron pilots, April 1945

310 Squadron mechanics, April 1945

Chapter 8: Czechoslovakia III

1945 September
By this time Czech B-24 Liberators, American bombers, were flying to England to fetch the numerous documents and books and other items stored at the offices of the Czech Government-in-Exile in London. I was advised to be on standby in Manston for a flight back on one of these. Eventually, I had to make a quick journey to another R.A.F. airport near London to catch my plane to Prague. Prior to this, I phoned Joan, who in the meantime had had to visit the Czech Repatriation Offices in London to get some further instructions regarding her train journey to Prague.

Our Liberator touched down around lunchtime on 23rd September at Ruzyně Airport in Prague. It was a very hot sunny day and it was Sunday. The airport looked deserted and I felt very lonely. However, the situation soon changed as I walked over the tarmac and was greeted by a friendly, welcoming smile. The officer was still in uniform and had been a member of the Czechoslovak 311 Squadron (bomber) in England. He also remembered me from early in 1940 when he was escaping from Czechoslovakia, staying at our house before crossing into Hungary. He was able to guide me and told me where I would be accommodated, at the Hotel Alcron, and arranged a taxi for me by giving the taxi driver a can of petrol! At that time petrol was strictly rationed. Most of the vehicles ran on wood gas.

Many of my friends, and others, were living at the hotel, all still looking for some suitable accommodation. It seemed that in the turmoil immediately after the end of the war people (especially those who had been in concentration camps as forced labourers and those who came back with the Russian army) had simply taken over all the empty properties and flats when the Germans were forced to leave the country. There was little chance of me finding any accommodation in Prague. I put my name down for a flat at the *Národní Výbor*, National Committee office in the Town Hall, hoping that they would allocate a flat for me before Joan arrived. I was given four weeks' leave and some Czech money and quickly proceeded by train to see my parents in Kotelszer Pusta. I still had my battledress with Flight Sergeant's stripes and still carried my colt. There were only a few trains running and they were all packed. Some of the coaches had no windows, there was no lighting and all the leather straps had been cut off – this was blamed on the Russian soldiers.

At Biskupice Pri Dunaji, the closest station to our home, the stationmaster Mr. J. Černil, who with his son Jaroslav and the rest of his family had actively helped escapees in 1939/40, welcomed me and arranged for his son to take me on his motorbike to my parents' home. It was a lovely reunion. There was such a lot to relate and explain after being away for just over five-and-a-half years. My parents were simply delighted that all three of us, Ludvík, Jaroslav and I, had been able to return home. However, they had some sad news for me about Ludvík, who had been caught by the Germans in Hungary in 1941. He had been a parachutist in the Russian army and had been interned in Mauthausen concentration camp until the end of the war. He had then rejoined the Czech army as an intelligence officer. While on duty in northern Bohemia he had been knocked off his motorbike by a Russian lorry, and he was now in hospital with very serious injuries. There was also another urgent matter – to arrange transportation, a lorry, for my parents' possessions. They had been allocated an empty house in Vojkovice, 15 kilometres south of Brno, vacated by the Germans when the Russian "liberators" came.

My parents were quite surprised that I had married an English girl and cautiously accepted the fact. I assured them that they would like her when she eventually arrived. I went back to Brno to arrange for a lorry. At that time all transport was regulated by the local *Národní Výbor*. With their authorization, a lorry, wood gas driven, and a driver were allocated to me and we set out for my parents' house in Slovakia. The following day, they and their possessions were moved to Vojkovice.

In my battledress uniform, with Flight Sergeant insignia and my colt showing at my side, I was able to move anywhere without hindrance. Some people even approached me, thinking that I was perhaps a policeman who could sort out their problems. I only stayed in the area for a few days, visiting friends and families in Biskupice and Alžbětín Dvor, and Karel Vaculík in Miloslavov. He had participated in my activities in 1939/40, guiding and taking escapees across the borders. In Bratislava I called on my ex-employers Jan Matys and his wife and my very good friend from the Commercial Academy, Alfred Kellner and his parents.

I also visited Mr. Knobloch, the manager of the Legio-Banka, Mr. Kopaček, the manager of the Živnobanka and Jur.Dr. Kubaček, the attorney of Živnobanka, who was in a very poor physical state, having returned from a concentration camp in Germany after many years of imprisonment. I also visited Professor Dr. J. Svozil, who was my form master at the Commercial Academy when I defected in February 1940. He was very apprehensive about the Russian "liberators". He said that the behaviour of the Russian soldiers was simply unacceptable to our civilized way of life. During one encounter with a quite high-ranking Russian officer, he had been under threat of being shot. He had been forced to sit down on a kerbstone for hours, drinking vodka with the officer – for the glory of the Russian motherland. Incidents like these happened quite frequently in Bratislava.

At last I was able to visit my brother Jaroslav. He had already been demobilized and was managing a grocery business in Bratislava, with the hope that he would be able to buy it. At that time, all properties, businesses, etc. which had been taken over from the Germans, collaborators and other internal enemies were looked after temporarily by managers with proven allegiance to the state, until they could afford to buy them for a nominal price. Jaroslav was very happy being in the trade for which he had been trained. Business was good and his future promising. He told me about his homecoming and the big celebration parade in Prague's Wenceslas Square on the arrival of the Czechoslovak Army.

On my return journey I called on my parents to see how they were settling down in Vojkovice. My eldest sister, Emilie, was still living with them. This was more or less a retirement place for my parents, with only a few acres of land and a small vineyard. My sister Božena, who was married to Richard Koubek, moved out of Slovakia with my parents and they were allocated a farm in Medlov after the Germans had been expelled from the area, only five or six kilometres away. Before the war, my sister Růžena had married František Mikulášek in Nosislav, about six or seven kilometres from Vojkovice. I was able to visit them and hear all about their life under the Germans during the Protectorate, how they helped by sending food parcels to my brother in Mauthausen concentration camp and their experiences with the Russians, the "liberators", when they were passing through the area.

October

As I urgently needed to find a flat in Prague, I cut short my stay in Bratislava and promised all my other friends that I would visit them sometime the following year. My application for a flat at the *Národní Výbor* offices in central Prague did not meet with any success. After daily visits to their office, I was referred to the Prague XII (Vinohrady) *Národní Výbor* office, where I was promised that I would be helped in this matter. My four weeks leave was now over and on 19th October I had to report to the Kbely Air Force Base to resume my duties. All the flying personnel and most of the ground personnel were ex-R.A.F. as were the officers in charge. Everything seemed to be in a process of reorganization, with new regulations etc. The day started early in the morning and finished by 3 or 3.30 p.m. This gave me time to pursue my search for a flat.

November

A message came that the repatriation train, with Joan and many others on board, was going to arrive at Prague *Wilsonovo nádraží* (Wilson Station) on 17th November. This was only five days away and I still did not have any accommodation for Joan. I pleaded with the official at the *Národní Výbor* to help me find a flat in their area, explaining the urgency. One evening, I called on the chairman of the *Národní Výbor*, a communist, and he listened to my desperate plight. He then helped me secure a flat at Řimská 42, Prague XII, which was being held by a Russian who was saving it for his girlfriend. With two days to spare, I managed to clean it and bring some furniture in from the *Národní Výbor* (they had warehouses with lots of confiscated German furniture, etc).

The flat was on the 1st floor in a new, modern, five-storey building with central heating, double-glazed windows, large living room, kitchen with electrical appliances, bathroom, separate WC, pantry and hall plus, in the basement, laundry facilities, washing machines, drying facilities etc. Unfortunately, as it had previously been occupied by Germans, you could still see the marks on the façade of the building after it had been sprayed with bullets during the Prague Uprising and some of the window panes were broken or missing. I even managed to buy a couple of plates, cups and saucers, and some knives and forks just in time!

The great day, 17th November, came: Joan was going to join me. However, there was a considerable delay before the repatriated wives were allowed to leave the train. It turned out that the train was also carrying representatives from numerous countries who were going to participate in the Prague World Gathering of Students. At last, I could see her waving to me from a window. It was lovely to see her and this time she would really be in my care. It was a most memorable reunion: there were so many things we wanted to hear about and share with each other.

Joan had travelled on a repatriation train with Laura Černohous, whose husband Jaroslav had been in the Czechoslovak Army in England. The whole journey from Manchester had taken five days and it had been quite an experience travelling through a devastated Germany. Joan had only brought a couple of suitcases; the rest of her dowry was packed in wooden boxes to follow as freight. I think Joan was very happy with our flat. We had to improvise with quite a few things like curtains, chairs, etc, things that were very hard to obtain, as everything was rationed and in very short supply. We also had to wait for some time to have our windows reglazed.

Food was rationed too. However, flying personnel were in the highest recipient category, with very generous allocations of *body*, coupons, for rationed goods. We were advised to use these sparingly, especially at the butchers, to avoid questions from other customers. Having a few days off from my duties, I took Joan to all the shops – the dairy, grocers, butchers, etc. – to introduce her to the managers and ask them to be understanding and helpful when Joan came to buy their goods. They were very happy to do so and Joan found them very co-operative.

At that time, her Czech was just about non-existent. I prepared a few helpful notes for her, to make it easier to ask for what she needed. She was generally known as *ta Angličanka*, the English lady. At first, our cuisine was quite plain as Joan's cooking experience was minimal. However, her skills soon improved, having such generous rations and having a free hand to experiment with them! Before long, Joan joined the British-born Wives' Club, which had been opened under the patronage of Lady Nicholls, the British ambassador's wife. She was very supportive and helpful, making it easier for the wives to get used to their new environment.

The British-born Wives' Club already had more than 100 members and was thriving. Members were able to exchange experiences, acquire new friends and thus find ways to cope with a multitude of problems. The club also arranged for anyone who wished to attend Czech cookery lessons and Joan and many others did. I was keen to complete my education at the Commercial Academy, and obtained permission from the Military Authorities to do so. I then approached the Commercial Academy in Prague to re-enrol. It turned out that I could study as a *privatista*, a private student, on a part-time basis, with classes every evening and on most Sunday mornings. My application was accepted and the head of the Academy arranged for me to have one of the brightest students for the duration of the course, to put me in the picture about the syllabus and to guide me in all the subjects required for my matriculation. His name was Karel Dušek. There were ten of us on this course. However, I was the only one whose studies had been interrupted by the war and had been actively fighting with the Czech forces abroad.

Joan must have found times very hard because of my absence in the evenings but agreed that it was the right thing to do, as qualifying would help me in my future career in the Air Force. My O.C. at Kbely Airbase was Lt.Col. Emil Foit whose wife, Joyce, was also English. As most of our flying duties were performed in the mornings, I was allowed to pursue my studies in a quiet room at the base in the afternoons. Life went on in a relaxed atmosphere: everyone was being given a chance to settle down and readjust to the new conditions. National service was reintroduced and many of the new recruits came to Kbely. Officers and NCO's who had been in active service prior to the war were readmitted to the Army and the Air Force, after being scrutinized by military tribunals. This meant that their activities during the German occupation, their character and their attitudes during that time were thoroughly investigated. A few of my friends were undecided about rejoining the armed services, but they were not hurried to make up their minds.

December
Joan and I made many friends, especially amongst the Air Force personnel who had English wives. Christmas was approaching and I was looking forward to introducing Joan to my parents in Vojkovice, and to my sisters Emilie, Růžena and Božena and my brothers Ludvík

and Jaroslav. I was given 14 days leave and we travelled to Vojkovice by train, via Brno. The journey was incredible: we were packed like sardines. My parents were delighted to meet Joan. So were my sisters and Jaroslav; Ludvík was still in hospital. The big problem now was how to communicate with Joan. However, the few words Joan had already learned helped a great deal. Of course, I was there all the time, helping to translate. There were so many questions and explanations regarding ways of life, Christmas celebrations, etc. How we had celebrated in England and now we were here in Vojkovice! Everyday was a feast. There was plenty of food, biscuits, cakes, and drink. Living in the country certainly had its advantages!

Visiting my parents' house must have been quite a novelty for Joan. Even the *peřina*, the feather-filled bed cover, was new and strange. We were introduced to quite a few of my parents' friends who came, I gather, to see Joan, *tu Angličanku*, and me – the airman! My parents gave us 30,000 Czech crowns as my part of the inheritance from the family farming business. We were absolutely delighted and quickly decided how we were going to spend it. First on the list was a new bed-settee and curtains for our flat in Prague. We had quite a job carrying all the food that we were given to take back with us. This was mostly meat (pork and poultry) preserved in fat in jars, all ready to eat. Back in Prague, we were recommended an interior designer who came and took measurements for our bed-settee and curtains. The order was to be delivered in eight weeks and when it came we were delighted.

1946 January – June
I continued my studies at the Commercial Academy, which occupied most of my free time and demanded a lot of concentration and effort from me to keep up. Karel Dušek, my mentor, was still a very great help. Joan was in frequent contact with her parents, who often sent her parcels with items that were unavailable in Czechoslovakia. However, she mostly waited for cigarettes, as the brand she liked was hard to obtain and was very expensive in Prague. The postman who delivered the packets always gave Joan a nice smile, as if knowing what was inside, and he was often rewarded with a cigarette.

Joan's mother and father were intending to visit us in Prague in the summer, so we had plenty of time to find accommodation for them, preferably in our district. Thanks to Joan's cookery lessons, our cuisine improved immensely and occasionally we even dared to invite some of our friends for a meal. At Kbely, life became a little bit strained with the introduction of new regulations. A political culture, a previously unknown phenomenon, also began to permeate military establishments. It was something completely new to all of us, as before the war our Army, which then included the Air Force, had always been non-political. Perhaps this was the first sign of Russian influence. In the May elections, the Communists won and Klement Gottwald became prime minister.

Joan's social life became more active, meeting new friends at the British-born Wives' Club. Eileen Scott and Norah (Brown) Vavřinek worked at the British Embassy and had moved into the house next to 42 Rimská Ulice where we lived, together with another couple of British consular staff, and we occasionally played bridge with them. On quite a few occasions we were asked to parties at the homes of other officers, including those of Lt.Col. Foit, Lt.Col. Vancl, Capt. Rostislav Kaňovský, Capt. Novotný, Capt. Piška and others. We also went to a party at the British Embassy on the occasion of the King's Birthday and represented the Czechoslovak Air Force at the Russian Military Attaché's party along with a few other officers.

The United Nations Relief and Rehabilitation Administration (UNRRA) was responsible for all-round improvements in food supplies. Many new items of food, such as frozen cod, appeared in the shops. However, no one knew what it was or even less how to cook it! It turned out that it was a great help to maintain a balanced diet and avoid malnutrition. One of the most appreciated items available via UNRRA was the American K-Ration Packs, which were frequently found on the black market because they also included cigarettes.

At Kbely, a few of my friends in my unit had decided to seek other careers – some took up civil occupations, some were employed by Czechoslovak Airlines and some were given control tower duties by the Ministry of Aviation; others went on to further education. Most of us, however, opted to stay in the Air Force and become career officers. My promotion to Second Lieutenant, *podporučík*, equivalent to Pilot Officer in the R.A.F. came on 4th March and was backdated to 1st January. In June, I successfully completed my studies at the Commercial Academy and presented my certificate to the Ministry of Defence for their appraisal. Shortly afterwards I was promoted to the rank of 1st Lieutenant, *nadporučík*, equivalent to Flying Officer in the

R.A.F. and was accepted for active service as a pilot in the Air Force. Joan and I were pleased with our prospects for the future.

July

Joan's mother and father came to see us in Prague. I had managed to find accommodation for them with a Czech family not far from where we lived. We were both delighted to see them again. I think that they were happy to see that we were coping with life reasonably well. Things around us were still not quite as clear-cut as in England, but there were signs that improvements would come soon!

Ludvík was making very good progress, recovering from his accident a year ago. I was asked to be his best man at his wedding to Milada from Pardubice (she was a cousin of Mít'a Čeřenský, who had also been interned in Mauthausen concentration camp with Ludvík). We all attended the ceremony at the Registry Office on Staroměstské náměstí in Prague. Joan's mother and father were quite busy every day, sightseeing, visiting museums, meeting a few of our friends and visiting F.O. František Vavřinek's family. He had been a pilot in 313 Squadron and had married Norah Brown from Bramhall, Stockport. Norah's mother had flown with Joan's mother and father to Prague, to visit her grandchild Michael. Now that Joan's mother and father had seen where and how we lived, it was not too painful to say goodbye and say that we would hopefully see them again soon.

I kept up my flying, with short flights almost daily. I was also selected to participate at air shows where we had realistic, though mock, attacks on ground targets and mock air combats. All the squadrons at Kbely participated in a Fly-Past at the Strahov Sokol Olympiad. I also started night flying in the autumn. I became a member of Czechoslovak Airmen's Club and the Czechoslovak Legionaries Club, both continuations of pre-war organizations. This year the Czech Legionaries held a national meeting in Prague, which culminated in a parade and march through the streets of Prague. Thousands of Legionaries expressed their dissatisfaction with the red tape they had encountered at the *Národní Výbor* offices, especially when looking for respectable accommodation, or even just making appointments to view flats, which were only obtainable with official permits from the *Národní Výbor*. Our parade met with the approval of the general public and tens of thousands of people applauded us. (Tens of thousands of Germans had left Prague in 1945 and all their houses and flats had been taken over by Communist Party members even before our Army and Air Force had arrived from the West.)

At one of our Airmen's Club meetings, a representative from the government came to explain the reasons for some of our new daily routines, asking us to be patient and to give the government a chance to bring matters back to normal. A few of my friends, who had come from Volyn in Eastern Poland and joined the Czechoslovak Forces in the Middle East, and later on the R.A.F, asked what was going on in that part of the country, because letters to their families had been unanswered. And, if a letter was answered, it took more than two months to arrive. Letters from England or Canada at this time took only five days. The representative could not give a satisfactory answer, except that the Russian communications must have been badly damaged during the war, and that he would make enquiries into the matter. Later, I found out that none of these friends had gone back to Volyn and many had emigrated or escaped from Czechoslovakia later on.

August – December
In August we were asked by the Air Ministry to participate in "voluntary" work on state-managed farms that had been left by the expelled Germans. This was called *brigáda* and applied to all the officers. This was a rather unusual request. It would have been understandable in an emergency, but was there an emergency now? In the event, it was only for four days.

There was constant bickering among the political parties, mainly because the communists were demanding more government posts and it seemed that the existing balance of power would remain until the next election. The communists had been given the Ministry of the Interior and in the beginning their powers were often abused, to the great dislike of all the other, democratic, parties. The unions were mostly dominated by communists, who agitated for a better future for all and proposed to achieve this by nationalizing all the private industries. This idea was hard to believe, especially for those of us who had fought during the War for the restoration of a democratic Czechoslovakia. Our hopes were still high that the majority of the nation would choose democracy for their future.

In the late summer, Joan realised that she was pregnant and became quite ill. On two or three occasions, I had to ask the doctors to examine her and give us their assurance that all was well. At the same time we were delighted with the news and realised that we would have to cut down on our social activities. At the base I kept up my flying routine and once a month took part in navigational flights, which qualified me for an additional increment in my salary. At about this time, night flying was also introduced, which I enjoyed very much. And we began to look for larger accommodation. We went to view a couple of flats with the hope of being able to make an exchange, however these efforts were unsuccessful.

A friend of mine, Štěpán Hall, also a *nadporučík*, invited us to his parents' house in Domažlice, south of Plzeň, for a weekend to go hare hunting. I even managed to shoot one. However, before we actually got to it, it nearly managed to run away! Unfortunately, neither Joan nor I knew how to skin it. After quite some time, we somehow managed to do it together. By then, with the help of a cookery book and attending Czech cookery lessons, Joan had made great advances in her cooking and managed to prepare a delicious meal. However, the whole experience put us off and there was no more hunting for either of us!

Joan was sorry when Norah Vavřínek had to move to Brno, to where her husband had been posted. We were invited again to the Měřička family for a meal. It was a splendid occasion and, of course, Otakar Machek was also there, courting their daughter Mirka. The meal was simply unforgettable – stuffed paprika with a rich cream sauce. Unfortunately, this made Joan very ill indeed. Later, just the sight of a paprika or the smell of it made her sick. We blamed the pregnancy! Shortly after our visit there I was asked by Otakar to come to the Měřička home again, this time to witness his asking for Mirka's hand from her father in the traditional way, by kneeling in front of him. The whole family was present. Otakar received Mirka's father's consent and we all drank their health to celebrate the occasion. The marriage was planned to take place early in the next year. By that time, Otakar had hoped to have completed his exams – he was studying medicine. (Otakar and Mirka were eventually married in March 1947 at St. Vitus Cathedral. I was their best man. The Bishop of Prague performed the ceremony and Joan even managed to attend the reception.)

Parcels from Joan's mother and father in England still arrived quite regularly, helping us with luxuries unobtainable locally. At

Christmas we went by train to visit my parents and the Vavřineks in Brno. This time I was able to reserve seats in a 2nd class compartment. However, the train was packed and not even the railway police were able to do anything about it. Eventually Joan was able to squeeze in and sit down for part of the journey. We called on the Vavřineks in Brno first and stayed there for two days. Their 3rd floor flat was simply luxurious with very large rooms, centrally heated and with double glazing. We certainly did envy them. Frank did most of the cooking and he was good at it; Norah had her hands full with their baby!

Visiting my parents was again a great occasion and this time with the news of Joan's pregnancy. The stay seemed to be a continual celebration and feast. Jarda (Jaroslav) also came for few days and was able to speak in English to Joan. We also managed to visit my sister Růžena and her family in Nosislav. My mother and sister Emilie were already trying to give some hints to Joan about the baby and how to look after it. I assured them that Joan would be capable of coping. We loaded up again with lots of jars of preserved meat (pork, chicken) and fruit and managed to get home safely to Prague. Considering all the upheaval, Joan had managed very well.

1947 January
Occasionally, the local doctor called to see Joan to see that all was well with the pregnancy. The weather had become extremely cold, 15 °C below, and there was lots of snow everywhere. We were advised not to use the hot water excessively, because the supplies of coke to centrally heated buildings had already been disrupted. The Vltava River was frozen to a depth of nearly half a metre and people were actually skating on it. Some of the schools were closed for lack of fuel for ten days. We were also without hot water and heating for three days before a new delivery of coke came. It was simply tipped against the front of the building. This time, everyone helped to get it into the cellar without grumbling, to the delight of the caretakers! The warmest place in our flat was the kitchen, as we had an electric cooker.

February
I was informed by the Bratislava Military Command that I had again been awarded the War Cross (*Válečný Kříž*) and the Military Medal

for Merit (*Medaile Za zásluhy*) by the President of the Czechoslovak Republic for my activities in connection with the liberation of our country, i.e. my underground activities taking escapees across the borders to Hungary and from Budapest to the Yugoslav borders, and I was invited to go to Bratislava for the public presentation on 7th March. However, I was told that I would have to pay my own expenses; I was not even offered the chance to accompany a higher ranking officer who had arranged official transportation for himself. I was both disappointed and angry at being treated this way and told my superiors that I would not be going to Bratislava, ostensibly because of Joan's pregnancy. The awards and citations were sent on to me by the Ministry of National Defence.

March – June
Early in March, Mrs. Lída Matys from Bratislava approached us about their daughter Lída and the possibility of arranging for her to go to England for a year to study at an English school. Joan wrote home to her parents to find out what to do and, of course, to find out whether there was somewhere she could stay.

Our preparations for the baby were in full swing. I managed to get a cot from the *Národní Výbor*. Joan had already received some clothing from England and from friends in Prague. The excitement was mounting for the big event. Joan felt very fit! On 22nd March she was taken to the Military Hospital in Střešovice and at 7.30 p.m. Anthony (Tony) Pavel was born. The news reached me at home by telephone (there was a joint phone in the hall). I could not stay at home, I just wanted to go out and celebrate and share my excitement with somebody but could not find anyone. Finally I had a few drinks alone. I also sent a telegram to Joan's parents in England.

I visited the hospital daily. Joan and the baby were doing well though she did not like the hospital food. After a few days Joan and the baby came home to our flat. Dr. Marie Hrušáková (the mother of my friend Ilja Hrušák, a pilot in 311 Squadron) came to see Joan and the baby. She also made arrangements for regular visits to her children's clinic, not far from our flat. Soon, visitors started to call, many of them bringing something for the baby. Being so small, 5½ lbs at birth, Tony had to be fed every two hours at the beginning and later every four hours, day and night. This was quite a task for Joan. I often had to wake Joan up when it was time. We had quite a few sleepless nights with Tony because of his feeding. His weight was a bit of a problem too. He was awake most of the time, which was so contrary to what the books and doctors had said. Mirka Měříček's parents gave Joan a few items of clothing for *Toníček*, Little Tony. My fourteen days leave came to an end. However, Joan was coping well with help from her friends who visited her regularly.

At Dr. Hrušáková's clinic Joan became a model mother, knowing how to look after and wrap up the baby – the local girls were accustomed to tying their blankets tightly around them. We were given an extra ration for the baby's needs, especially milk which we had to collect from a nearby dairy. Joan soon made her mind up to go to England in the summer, to show the baby to her parents and the friends she had left behind. We agreed that July would be about right and Joan wrote home to tell everyone. In the meantime, lots of congratulations and parcels arrived from England. We also had a letter from Joan's parents about Lída Matys being accepted to start at Levenshulme High School in September. We wrote to her parents about the good news, and Joan's parents generously said that Lída would be able to stay with them until the end of the year. In April I was asked to be best man at the wedding of my friend Štěpán Hall, who was going to marry a local girl, Jarmila, at Kbely.

With all the excitement and preparations for going home to England, time seemed to pass very quickly. We thought that it would be a good idea for Lída Matys to accompany Joan in July. Her parents were delighted with these arrangements. We managed to withdraw money from our "frozen account" to buy a new pram: in 1945 all savings had been frozen and a new currency had been introduced. One could only change a minimal amount, enough to last until you received your next monthly salary. Permission to use the frozen account could only be obtained in an emergency and only with a very good reason.

It was generally known at this time that most of the flying personnel were going to be moved to Hradec Králové, where a new flying academy was going to be established. Quite a few of my friends did not like the idea of moving out of Prague, where they had settled down, enjoying life in the capital. However, only a very few decided to leave the Air Force and seek other employment. The date for the move was set for the beginning of May. When the orders came I was pleasantly surprised that my name was not on the list. I was appointed adjutant to Lt.Col. František Fajtl, who became the O.C. of the newly created mobilisation unit at Kbely. Joan and I were delighted that we would not have to move out of Prague.

A Russian, who lived in a flat in our block was seen on occasion loading his Jeep with carpets and other items of furniture, collected from the empty dwellings of Sudetenland Germans.

July

The eagerly awaited time came and Joan, Tony and Lída Matys departed for England. I had planned to make use of this opportunity to spend my holidays visiting Bratislava and all my friends there and also to call on my parents in Vojkovice. In Bratislava I was invited to stay with Mr. and Mrs. Matys, and Mrs. Matys suggested a trip to the High Tatras in a large chauffeur-driven American car. (The car belonged to the company in which her husband was a partner.) I agreed to accompany them, as I had never visited that region of Slovakia before. It was a marvellous experience, seeing such beautiful countryside – the lakeside resort of Štrbské Pleso, the stalactite cave at Lomnický Štit and the 2655 m high Gerlachovka Mountain. I hoped I would be able to visit this part of the country again. After five most enjoyable days we returned to Bratislava.

I was invited to call on Mr. Vaclav Linhart, a wholesale importer of fruit in Bratislava, who had also worked in the underground movement and helped escapees to reach the French Consulate in Budapest in 1939/40. Prior to my escape from Slovakia on 19th February 1940, he had been able to visit Budapest and contact Mr. O. Šalek, the manager of a local bank who was also involved in helping escapees. Unfortunately, I was unable to visit Jur.Dr. Kubáček, who was still in hospital, recuperating after his release from a concentration camp in 1945. Mr Kopaček, the manager of another bank, was away the day I called. I also visited my friend Alfred Kellner and his parents. They were rather worried about the political situation and wondered what was going to happen to them. My friend Alfred had finished his studies and had gained a degree in engineering.

After a brief call at Vojkovice to see my parents, I returned to Prague to resume my duties. Only a day or two after my return I received a phone call from General Hanuš, from the Ministry of National Defence, and was again ordered to participate with a group of other officers in gathering in the harvest in the northern part of Bohemia, in an area from where the Germans had been expelled. I pointed out to the General that my O.C, Lt.Col. Fajtl, was still on holiday and that I would be unable to participate. However, the General told me that his order stood and I was obliged to go.

August – December
In August, Joan and Tony arrived back in Prague. It was so good to hear how much she had enjoyed her visit to her parents and meeting all her relations and friends. It was a simply unforgettable occasion and I was very happy just to sit and listen to all her experiences. In the limelight, of course, was the baby, Tony. Joan had managed to bring back a carrycot for him, and this became the focus of great interest when going anywhere, travelling on trams etc, as people had never seen anything like it before. I was able to pass on the news about Lída Matys and the arrangements that had been made for her schooling and accommodation to her parents in Bratislava, after hearing all the details from Joan. Otakar Machek finished his medical studies and applied to go to the U.S.A. for further studies. Permission was granted. However, he was not allowed to take Mirka, his wife, with him. In the autumn, Mirka managed to travel to Canada to visit friends and later joined Otakar in the U.S.A.

Joan, on one of her frequent visits to the local park with Tony in the pram, met a new English girl, Marjorie, originally from Birmingham, who was married to George Falkenau, who was in the Czech Army during the war. She also had a baby, Jennifer. We became good friends and visited each other whenever possible. They had a car and we appreciated going on outings with them to sights around Prague and to the countryside. George had a jewellery and watch business, import and export, which had belonged to him before the war.

To qualify for my pilot salary increment I had to keep up my flying, both daytime and night-time, and log a minimum number of hours each month. Fortunately, I was still able to fly with the unit stationed at Kbely.

We managed to attend numerous social occasions, mostly given by Air Force friends and others who had married English wives. However, Tony had to accompany us in his carrycot. At parties held in our flat he always managed to stay awake, regardless of how late they went on. Quite often, I was invited to play cards, *mariáš*, with my superior officers – Lt.Col. Emil Foit, Lt.Col. František Vancl, Staff Capt. Josef Sehnal – either in the afternoon after work or in the evenings at Emil Foit's home (sometimes until midnight!).

Joan was unable to visit the British-born Wives' Club, having to attend to Tony's needs. However, there were a few friends from the Club who would call and have a good chat with her. There were times when Joan had her hands full with Tony, especially when he was teething. Dr. Hrušáková was always very helpful and ready to help, whatever the reason.

Politically, the situation had still not been resolved. The communists were pressing very hard and demanding greater participation in the government. The Democratic parties managed to stave them off again for a while. We hoped that they would do so in the future too!

In order to rehabilitate officers who had remained in the country during the war, the Ministry of National Defence created a commission consisting of officers who would assess those seeking rehabilitation as to their behaviour and activities between 1938 and 1945, and appraise their deeds. I was asked to be a member of this commission. Each of the officers had to submit a written statement about their activities, a sort of CV. The Commission, comprising six to eight members, consisted of Colonels down to 1st Lieutenant, which was my rank.

One day in the autumn, Emil Foit asked me to join him in a business proposition together with Josef Sehnal and Jaroslav Kozelka (ex-R.A.F. F.O. now demobbed). Emil Foit's relation, Josef Machek from Holesov in Moravia, had come to inform us that there was a small garment factory in Holesov that was being run by managers appointed by the *Národní Výbor* and it would be possible for us to buy it, having a preferential option in these matters because of our wartime record. Josef Machek would become the manager and run it on our behalf. After discussing the matter with Josef, the present manageress had already agreed to support our acquisition of the factory and she was willing to stay on in charge of personnel. After a very lively discussion we agreed to go ahead with the matter. Our next meeting was arranged and held in a solicitor's office. The initial steps were discussed with the solicitor, about how to proceed after having had all the legal points explained to us. We were then to meet at a later date, to give the solicitor time to prepare the necessary documents for our partnership. Despite various new government regulations, the solicitor informed us that everything was still OK, with only some red-tape delays slowing down the process. However, it was already becoming apparent that the political climate had become somewhat difficult. Eventually, we all decided to cancel our involvement in the project.

At one of our Czechoslovak Airmen Association meetings we were most pleased to be able to welcome an unexpected guest – Jan Masaryk, the Minister of Foreign Affairs. He gave us a very frank lecture about the situation in the Czechoslovak Republic, especially concerning our new "friendship" with the U.S.S.R. and our future aspirations for a free democracy. He promised to do his utmost to guide Czechoslovak policy so as not to offend our "friends" in the East, but he also realised that it was only question of time before the "big bear" would pounce on us, being only a little mouse, at least as far as they were concerned. We all hoped that our leadership would skilfully avoid creating such an adverse situation. However, many of us were seriously shaken by his remarks and all sorts of thoughts went through our minds. Some of my friends, who had come from Eastern Poland, now occupied by Russia, and who had joined our Air Force during the war decided to leave Czechoslovakia, emigrating mostly to Canada, Australia and England. Their instinct to do so proved correct.

It must also be remembered that when the Marshall Plan, i.e. American aid to help countries with their economy, was first discussed earlier in the year the Czechoslovak Government initially opted to consider aid. However, after having visited Moscow for consultations, the Czech ministers had to officially refuse any help. To all of us this had seemed like interference by Russia in our democratic way of life. However, we still hoped that with President Beneš and our coalition government we would survive and overcome future problems. With Gottwald, a communist, as prime minister and the Ministry of the Interior in communists' hands, there were signs, mostly via reports in the press, that they were abusing their powers, especially by introducing new regulations which were in direct conflict with the law. Yet nothing was done about it. At meetings with our friends we openly discussed the prevailing situation in the country. However, there was no sign which way the Army would react to it all, should a critical situation arise. We now became very conscious of all these unwelcome events.

At our flat we noticed that our caretaker, Mrs. Brož, was paying keen attention to us, to our visitors and even listening to Joan's telephone calls (the telephone was situated in the hall). I knew that she was a communist.

There were all sorts of rumours going around and doubts about the regime crept into our minds. Most of us believed that the Army (which included the Air Force) would eventually have the final say and stop fierce quarrels among the political parties and defend our democratic system. Up till now, we had had very little news from military sources about these matters.

We decided not to visit my parents for Christmas. We thought that with Tony still being a baby, it would perhaps be too much for my parents to look after all of us. My parents were very disappointed and hoped that we would be able to see them early in the spring. In the meantime, Ludvík, who had visited them, brought us lots of jars of preserved cooked meats and other treats, specially baked for Christmas, such as *pusinky-perničky*, gingerbread meringues. Joan received 'The Parcel' from her parents, which was always greatly appreciated. There was also a letter giving us all the news from home and about Lída, who was living with them, and the very good progress she was making learning English at her new school.

During the Christmas holidays quite a few friends came to see us, and we celebrated with all the treats that my parents had sent to us and the wine that I was able to purchase through our military unit allocation. We even managed to put up a small Christmas tree! To welcome in the New Year, we were invited to Marjory and George Falkenau who lived in a flat not far away, taking Tony with us, sleeping in his carrycot. We listened to Radio Luxemburg, whose programmes were mostly broadcast for the entertainment of American forces in Germany. The song they seemed to play a lot, and which then appealed to me, was: "I don't want her, you can have her, she's too fat for me!" George was wondering what would happen to his business, should things deteriorate politically as it had not been completely handed back to him. He was only allowed to run it as an appointed administrator. On our way home we could hear music from the cafés and restaurants. Sylvester, the last day of the year, was always a great celebration and parties often lasted for hours into the New Year.

I had previously applied for a Civil Airlines Pilot's Diploma – a pilot's licence – and it was issued to me on 31st December 1947.

1948 January – February
In January, at the Czechoslovak Legionaries meeting held at *Národní dům,* National House on Vinohradské náměstí, the attendance was exceptionally large. Everyone wanted to hear from the chairman what was happening in the country and what attitude and precautions we would be taking. The speaker, Lt.Col. Bedřich Reicin, who had come on behalf of the Ministry of Defence, failed to pacify us with his unconvincing explanations. Too many questions remained unanswered. It looked as though the Army was not going to commit itself in the prevailing critical political situation. (The Czechoslovak Legionaries comprised ex-servicemen who had participated in fighting against the enemies of the state as well as those who were now in active service, regardless of their rank.) Disheartened with the outcome of this meeting, we all wondered what sort of a future we could expect.

The free press reported daily about numerous transgressions committed by the Unions, *Uro,* which were firmly run by the communists. However, the most worrying part was that they had been organizing themselves into a "Workers' Militia", and a cache of arms had been discovered. With the Ministry of the Interior in communist hands, all this was either tolerated or just denied. Bickering and mistrust between the non-communist ministers and the ministers of the communist party reached a climax one day in the second half of February: the cabinet ministers of the non-communist parties resigned, as they were not prepared to put up with the pressure of communist demands.

Prime Minister Gottwald forced President Beneš to let the largest political party, the communists, take power and form a government. Jan Masaryk, the Foreign Secretary, being non-political, was retained by the communists. All other political party offices, and their press, were closed immediately with the exception of those of the social democrats, who allied themselves with the communists. All the unions publicly demonstrated in the streets of Prague in support of the takeover. Many of them were armed, calling themselves the "Workers' Militia".

The following day when I went to work, I was quite surprised to be told that I was not allowed to go into the airport area at Kbely. However, I could still carry on with my duties at the administration buildings. The prohibition applied to all ex-R.A.F. flying personnel. This was the final straw. I realised then that our country's democratic system had become totally suppressed and that our fight and efforts to preserve it had failed. Joan and I discussed all our options and came to the conclusion that we might have to leave the country. The Air Ministry arranged a meeting, as all ex-R.A.F. servicemen had demanded further explanations and wanted to know what was going to happen in the future. We were told that we were soon to be reorganized and that a "clean up" in the armed forces would take place. Quite simply, we were classified as unreliable elements, especially those of us who had married British or other foreign girls. Some of the ex-R.A.F. officers who had married Czech girls after the war demanded to be allowed to fly and carry out their duties. They were told that for the time being this would not be allowed either. It appeared that those who wanted to stay in the Air Force had to join the communist party, thus betraying all the principles we stood for and had fought for. My mind was made up – I was going to leave!

Lots of my officer friends, mainly those who had British-born wives, came to see me, wondering how we were going to organize an escape. However, one could not completely trust everyone who had served during the war in the West, because those who had married locally did not want to leave the country again, having settled down with their families. They were prepared to face the future here, whatever was going to happen. A group of us with British-born wives – Captains Jaroslav Šlepica, Josef Jílek, Alois Piška and myself – were extremely cautious when we arranged to meet at our flat to discuss the possibility of an escape. And we all had families, making it a rather complicated and very dangerous matter. We arranged to meet again the following week, hoping to come up with some ideas for our plan. In the meantime, questions were being asked by foreign correspondents and the British Embassy about what would happen to British-born wives. Prime Minister Gottwald declared that the country was not interested in British-born wives and those who wished to leave now could do so legally. Joan had friends at the British Consulate – she played cards with them – and went to see the British Consul to find out whether it would be possible for all three of us to leave for England. However, as I was still serving in the armed forces there was no way I could leave the country legally. The only way to leave would be to escape.

The advice Joan was given was that I should leave the country before she left with Tony. The Embassy and Consulate assured Joan that they would look after her and the baby. This was very useful information and I was able to proceed with my plans. At my office at Kbely I was able to find a possible route for my escape among the classified maps. I then simply cut out the part of the map I intended to use. This would be useful for our planning meeting. However, there was another obstacle to overcome. It was reported that an area within twenty kilometres of the borders was out of bounds for everyone, except those who lived there, and frequent spot checks were carried out on the passengers travelling in the area on trains or buses. Jaroslav Šlepica and Josef Jílek, then stationed in Brno, came up with a new escape idea: we would just take some Spitfires and fly west. They said that this would be possible as they had to go to Letňany, close to Kbely Airport, to collect Spitfires which were there for repairs. They promised to let me know about the date. Alois Piška was not at this meeting.

Joan's parents wrote to us, wondering if we were all right, as the developing political situation had been widely publicized all over the world. They even telephoned and Joan had assured them that we were managing, as we could not divulge anything about our intentions on the phone or in writing. At the end of February I managed to travel to Bratislava to see Mr. and Mrs. Matys and to tell them about our intentions, and find out what they wanted to do about their daughter Lída at school in England. They too were thinking of leaving the country and asked us to tell Lída to stay and wait for further instructions. I also called on my brother Jaroslav, who was managing a grocer's shop, and told him about my intentions. He was prepared to do likewise.

Mr. and Mrs. Matys asked me to see their friend Mr. Linhart, who still had his fruit import business in Bratislava. He was also rather worried about the political situation and thought that it would help him, should the situation deteriorate, to have a statement from me regarding his help in underground work in 1939/40, when escapees were leaving the country. I signed a statement to that effect and gave it to him. Mrs. Matys visited us shortly afterwards and helped us dispose of some items from our flat. Joan's friends from the Consulate also bought some items from us – crockery, cutlery, etc. Quite often, Eileen Scott visited us in the evenings, informing us about the latest developments. Eventually I was able to leave all my papers, documents, etc. with her and these were later sent to us in Manchester. During a casual discussion with my O.C, Lt.Col. Fajtl, I was asked what I intended to do and about my family. I informed him that I didn't have any other option than to leave the country. He said that he understood my predicament. He had also served in the R.A.F. and in Russia, and hoped that the "clean up" would not affect him. (He was dismissed in February 1948 and arrested in 1950, and served seventeen months in a labour camp. He was reinstated in 1989.)

March

The situation became even bleaker on 10th March when Jan Masaryk was found dead under the window of his apartment in Prague Castle. According to the press he had committed suicide. It was very hard to believe that he would have done anything like that!

I often met up with my closest friends to try and work out the best possible route for our escape. A few other friends had managed to find guides who had promised to take them over the borders into the American zone in Germany. However, they were demanding a great deal of money, between twenty and forty thousand crowns, an amount that I did not have. A few of them did find reliable guides, perhaps even cheaper, but the routes were getting crowded and there was a long waiting list. And, of course, there was always the risk of being discovered.

At one of my meetings with Emil Foit, who was also waiting for his turn to get across the border, he told me that one of his relations, Josef Machek (not related to Otakar Machek), whom I had already met, was also intending to escape. The route was via the town of Aš in the most westerly part of Czechoslovakia, and he was planning to go with his wife and another ex-R.A.F. friend. Josef's friend Mr Bartoš, who was then serving as a Customs and Excise border guard in that area, would take them across to Germany. Josef also knew a textile manufacturer, Mr Růžička, who lived in Aš and had a factory in the town. He also knew about Josef's intentions. I met Josef in Prague and I was able to arrange for Jaroslav and myself to be included in his party. However, we all had to get to Aš and were going to need good reasons for getting travel permits. Josef arranged with Mr Růžička to provide us all with documents that confirmed our employment in his factory. After discussing all the details with Josef, we set the date and the time when we would all meet in Prague and take the train to Aš. Having all the details finalized, I decided to take nine days leave, ostensibly to visit my parents.

On a leave pass form for officers, I filled in all the necessary details, including the main stations and my final destination: Prague-Brno-Vojkovice-Prague. After my pass had been signed and authorized, I added Aš to the list, as an extra precaution. I then told my brother all the details – when we were to meet in Prague, which train to take, etc. He promised to be there on time. The date for our journey to Aš was set for 27th March. My leave pass was valid from Saturday 20th March until Monday 29th March inclusive. Almost daily, there was news about people being caught trying to escape across the borders to Austria or to the American zone in Germany. Fatalities were also reported. A few days before the 27th, Jaroslav Šlepica came to inform me that he and Josef Jílek had been authorized to collect two Spitfires from Letňany and fly them back to their unit in Brno. However, it turned out that there were three Spitfires belonging to their unit ready for collection. They thought that this would be a good opportunity for me to collect the third one. I was not happy with their proposition, as I was then officially on leave and my home base was Kbely. I did not want to take any unnecessary risks and perhaps endanger us all. Later, after collecting their Spitfires, they flew west to the American zone in Germany.

I badly needed to get hold of a greatcoat for my journey. I only had military greatcoats, which, of course, were unsuitable. A couple of days before my departure, I met Mr Měřička on Wenceslas Square, one of the main squares in Prague. He very kindly arranged for me to collect a greatcoat from one of the shops where he knew the manager. I promised that I would repay him sometime for this very generous deed. He also informed me that his daughter Mirka had managed to get to the U.S.A. and was now with her husband Otakar. Mr. Měřička was rather worried about Otakar being able to look after her.

A few British-born wives who were leaving for England were turned back at the airport. Their British passports were not accepted by the authorities and they were told that they would have to apply for Czechoslovak passports. This, of course, would most probably apply to Joan and Tony as well, and delay our plans. Joan and I continued to discuss everything in detail. My main worry was what would happen to Joan and Tony should I get caught. Deserting whilst on active service was a very serious matter. However, I had to take this step, with the hope of surviving and building up our lives again. One evening we managed to smuggle some of our crockery to Eileen Scott in Tony's pram, well camouflaged as we did not want our caretaker, Mrs. Brož, to become suspicious about our intentions.

On Wednesday, 31st March, Joan was going to phone my office at Kbely to inform them that I was ill (we wrote it down in Czech – *Muj manžel je nemocný*, my husband is ill). We hoped that by then, if she had not heard from anyone, that I would be safely across the border.

Joyce Foit, the wife of Emil Foit, brought us the good news that her husband had managed to get across safely. Joyce now visited Joan and Tony every day and, of course, having Eileen Scott nearby and all her friends at the consulate, kept Joan's morale high. On Thursday 25th March I said good-bye to Joan and Tony. I was in civilian clothes but took a revolver with me that I had acquired from my father some time ago (I had a military permit to carry one), and left for the railway station to meet the others. To my surprise, there were more of us in the group than originally planned. Josef Machek assured me that we would be all right, as everyone had a work permit. And once we had arrived in Aš, we would be looked after by Mr. Bartoš, the Customs and Excise officer. Our group consisted of Josef Machek (factory manager from Moravia) and his wife Vlasta; Karel Bednařík (ex-R.A.F.) and his wife Andělka; Vojtěch Rygal, a Roman Catholic Priest; Jaroslav Kratochvíl (ex-Czechoslovak Army in England), and myself, 1st Lieutenant on active service (ex-R.A.F.).

We were lucky travelling on the train to Aš; no one asked us why we were on our way to that particular destination. However, on our arrival in Aš, we were informed that Mr. Bartoš, who was going to take us across the borders, had had to escape himself, together with his family and some other officers. They had taken their rifles with them as well. Apparently, the authorities had found out about their activities and were going to arrest them. The only thing we could do now was to meet Mr. Havelka, the manufacturer, and see what help we could get. Mr. Růžička gave us food and accommodated us for the night and also informed us that some new young Customs and Excise officers were taking over the border duties, and that these men were great sympathizers with the new regime.

The following day, Friday 26th, I decided that whatever happened I was going to make my way across the border, even if I had to do it without help. The others were prepared to follow me. I studied the map cutting that I had brought with me and got further guidance from Mr. Růžička as to the layout of the area and other useful information regarding the routines, etc. of the border guards. Mr. Havelka said that he expected a guide, a German girl from the American zone, to call on him that evening. We had planned to cross around midnight. About an hour before our departure, the German girl came to see him. Her own crossing of the border had been uneventful. It appeared that she knew the way well. But when we asked her to guide us back across the border, she refused. We were very disappointed and suspicious, wondering what she was really up to. However, she volunteered to guide us to a lonely barn out in the fields from where she told us about some of the obstacles we might encounter and how far it was between useful landmarks.

It was just after midnight, between Friday and Saturday, when all seven of us set out on our journey towards freedom. The girl also showed us which direction to follow to cross the border and how to find a lone farmhouse on the German side with a light in one of the rooms. We managed to cross the first two or three hundred metres, crouching and moving quietly and reached a railway line. It was a very bright night with a full moon shining and visibility was good. We all rested and listened for any signs of noise for about five minutes. We couldn't hear anything – except for the pounding of our hearts! As pre-arranged, we were going to cross the railway line on my signal in a single line abreast. After taking only a couple of steps, one of us tripped on a rail. The reverberating noise rang out in the night. Instantly, automatic weapons opened fire in our direction from the right, possibly from only about seventy metres away. We heard some swearing too! Then we heard someone shouting *stůj*, halt! I was determined to make a dash, regardless of the shooting.

Being a good runner, I just set off in the direction we had previously planned. After getting about a hundred and fifty metres away from the railway line, I looked behind me but could only see one other person about ten metres away following me. It was Josef Machek. At that moment I had no idea where the others were. Josef told me that it had looked as though all the tracer bullets were hitting me, but somehow I had managed to run like a ghost! We both now ran together for another two or three hundred metres, until we reached a wooded area with a lot of undergrowth of bracken and grass. We could hear the border guards shooting, now to our left. Originally, we had agreed that in the event of any shooting or a confrontation, we would disperse. We both hoped that these last rounds had not been aimed at anyone from our group. We then decided to lie low for a while, as we did not know exactly where the demarcation line was.

After about fifteen or twenty minutes we could hear the guards talking and walking in the direction of the guard house, which was to our right. They also had a dog, on a leash, with them. They must have been only about forty or fifty metres ahead of us, crossing our intended path into Germany. From their excited conversation, we could deduce that someone had been shot during the escape. After another five minutes, when we could no longer hear anything or anybody, we carefully moved forward. We found the demarcation post, but still made our way very carefully, knowing that the Czech border guards might shoot at us, even though we were already on the German side. Josef told me that his wrist or arm was aching terribly. Apparently, he had broken it a few weeks before and all this commotion had aggravated its condition. However, this problem would have to wait until we reached our destination. After walking for about half an hour, we saw the lonely farm and a light shining in one of its windows. Josef, who spoke German quite well, approached the front door and knocked. After some time a woman appeared and explained to us that we would have to report to the German border guards. We just could not believe that we would have to return to the official border crossing!

It took us almost an hour to get there and as we approached the building we could see that it was then only about fifteen metres to the Czechoslovak road barrier, fifteen metres between freedom and a jail sentence! After a brief interrogation and some form-filling, I surrendered my revolver to the German border guards. They then made some phone calls to the Americans and told us that we would have to wait for someone from the American authorities to come and pick us up. We were given coffee and sandwiches. By this time it was dawn. The German guards learned from the Czechoslovak guards what had happened that night. They were told that Vojtěch Rygal had been killed and the other four in our group had been caught. Jaroslav had been caught not far from where the priest had been shot. Karel Bednařík, his wife Andělka and Vlasta Machek had been caught while crossing the railway line. It was only then that we fully realised how lucky we had been and wondered what would happen to those who had been caught.

Eventually, a G.I. came in a jeep to take us to the nearby town of Hof, where an American HQ was situated. We were given lunch and in the afternoon one of their intelligence officers took us to be interrogated, individually. It was obvious to me that they were extremely well informed about the happenings in Czechoslovakia. However, this officer thought that he might need to speak to me again next day. We were given overnight accommodation and food and were quite happy to enjoy their hospitality. The next day, however, I was told that they would not need to see me and that we were going to be sent on to Schwabach, about twelve kilometres south of Nuremberg, where a DP, displaced persons, camp was located. Having brought some German money with us, we bought our own tickets and travelled there by train. All the DP camp refugees, including children, were accommodated in a big, empty factory. There were no beds but everybody had been issued with blankets. There must have been at least two hundred refugees there.

We soon found out where Mr Bartoš and his family were and he explained the situation he had been confronted with and what had led up to it. He was sorry to hear about the others from our group who did not make it. The routine in the DP camp was incredible. We were given *ersatz*, substitute, coffee three times a day and just 100 grams of bread. The coffee tasted as though it had been made of boiled socks. Most of the DP's had brought German currency with them, just as we had done, and were able to supplement these very meagre rations. Everyone was photographed and issued with a German *Kennkarte*, Identity Card.

April – May

There was not much to do in the DP camp. However, the problem now was for everyone to register and fill in an application form for admission to a country which you wanted to travel to. Thus began a slow process. Perhaps the shortest waiting times were for those who had relations in their country of choice as they would then become guarantors regarding their well-being and employment. Many DP's had no one to ask to be their guarantor and had to wait a long time until a country would accept them. As a rule, it was easier for young people without a family, or with desirable profession qualifications, to get permits. These sessions, however, were only conducted on certain days at the camp and there was a strict limited quota. Josef Machek put his name down for a permit to go to the U.S.A.

Two days after our arrival at the camp I decided to travel to Frankfurt to visit the British Consulate. Josef came with me. I filled in my application form for a visa to travel to the U.K. I was told that this would take a few days and to call back a week later for further news. We both went to the Red Cross HQ that had been set up for refugees and Josef was given a note to go to a German hospital to have his arm seen to and it was immediately put in plaster. Life at the camp carried on very slowly and bordered on hopelessness. The sanitation and washing facilities were very poor. To me this was a very painful and incredible situation. Imagine being looked after by Germans who, until recently, had been our enemies and who had lost the war. Still, I was sure that quite soon I was going to be able to join Joan and Tony in England.

My next visit to the British consulate was on 9th April. I was given a letter from the visa section telling me that my application had been sent to London and that I would be informed in due course. I wrote a letter to Joan, hoping that by then she had managed to leave Czechoslovakia, explaining to her what steps I had taken at the Consulate. While visiting the Consulate, I met Emil Foit, who was also waiting for his visa to the U.K. He was actually billeted in a compound that was under direct American care and where there were many high ranking officers. I was told that a Czechoslovak Consular Section was still in existence in Frankfurt and that they had refused to surrender their office to the new communist regime. I was advised to apply immediately for a temporary passport, which would then be valid for travel to the U.K. or, in fact, anywhere in the world. Without delay, I called on them and was issued with a temporary passport.

Towards the end of April, not having heard from the British Consulate, I called again to see whether my visa had arrived. It was very disappointing to be told that nothing had come yet from London. There were quite a few of us, mostly pilots, who were in similar circumstances. One of them told us that, according to an article in the press, the Turkish government was seeking pilots for their air force and perhaps we should consider this option if the British government refused our visa applications. There was no immediate response to this but the idea did linger on in the back of our minds. One week later, I called at the British Consulate and was again told that there was no news from London. Then, while sitting in the waiting room, I read in a local English bulletin, that the R.A.F. Association had recently opened a new branch in Frankfurt. Inquiries were to be made to Flt.Lt. W. Girdler. I contacted him there and then, from the British Consulate, and was invited to go and see him.

As I was the first Czechoslovak pilot to contact him, he arranged for me to be looked after by the British Repatriation Commission at Höchst, near Frankfurt. I was simply jubilant! The DP camp conditions, with barely any food, had left their mark on me. I had lost a lot of weight and my fingernails were cracked, a sure sign of malnutrition. The following day I said goodbye to Josef and travelled to Höchst to my new quarters. It was marvellous! I was allocated a room of my own and all the meals were served in the same building. The Mess President introduced me to all their members, about sixty or seventy people, men and women, though they were quartered elsewhere. I was well received and treated by everyone, all wishing me a speedy return to the U.K. and my family.

Occasionally, members of the Commission took me to the American PX store and bought me toiletries. They also took me on a few weekend drives out into the country. On Saturdays, socials were held in the mess. I felt very much in debt for all the generous treatment they gave me and felt rather uncomfortable about it all, as I was now penniless. To my great delight, I received a letter from Joan, briefly informing me about her getting home to Manchester. On one occasion, when I was taken to an American Servicemen's Club, I was introduced to the Provost Marshall, the senior military police officer of Frankfurt, by my escort from the British Repatriation Commission. He also obviously knew about the situation in which the Czechoslovak refugees found themselves. He told me to inform his office when my visa came through and he would make arrangements for my repatriation and would fly me over in one of their military aircraft based at Wiesbaden. This certainly boosted my morale. However, I was still waiting for my visa.

On my next visit to the British Consulate, I could see that quite a few young Jewish men were collecting their visas to go to the U.K. The odd thing was that they had never been to the U.K. before, or had any connections there, yet they were being granted visas, as it appeared, almost instantly. We later found out that they were en route to Israel. We felt terribly hurt, knowing what was going on; we had our wives and families in the U.K. and our wartime service did not seem to count for anything.

When, by the end of May, we had still not received our visas, our indignation was at its highest. Some of us were seriously considering finding out more about the possibility of joining the Turkish Air Force. Two high-ranking officers were going to find out more and inform us about the conditions of employment. The results of their enquiries never reached me because when I phoned Joan at the beginning of June and expressed my frustration with all the waiting for a visa, and the possibility, perhaps, of joining the Turkish Air Force, she promised to travel to London – to the Home Office – to find out why my visa was not forthcoming. Joan's involvement certainly worked. My visa was granted on 4th June and I was then able to make arrangements with the American military for a flight to the U.K. I was delighted with all this news, with high hopes of being able to rejoin my family in the near future.

Legionaries marching through Prague in 1946

My parents' house in Vojkovice

Ludvík's wedding in July 1946: Major Čeřenský, Horace Bitton, Ludvík Kratochvíl, Miladka, Miloslav Kratochvíl, Helen Bitton, Joan Kratochvíl

Spitfire air display team at Pardubice:
1st Lt. Štěpán Holl, 2nd Lt. Vladimír Nedělka, ...(mechanic),
Capt. Josef Novotný, Lt.Col. Emil Foit, Capt. Zdeněk Škarvada,
1st Lt. Miloslav Kratochvíl

In Prague, 1947

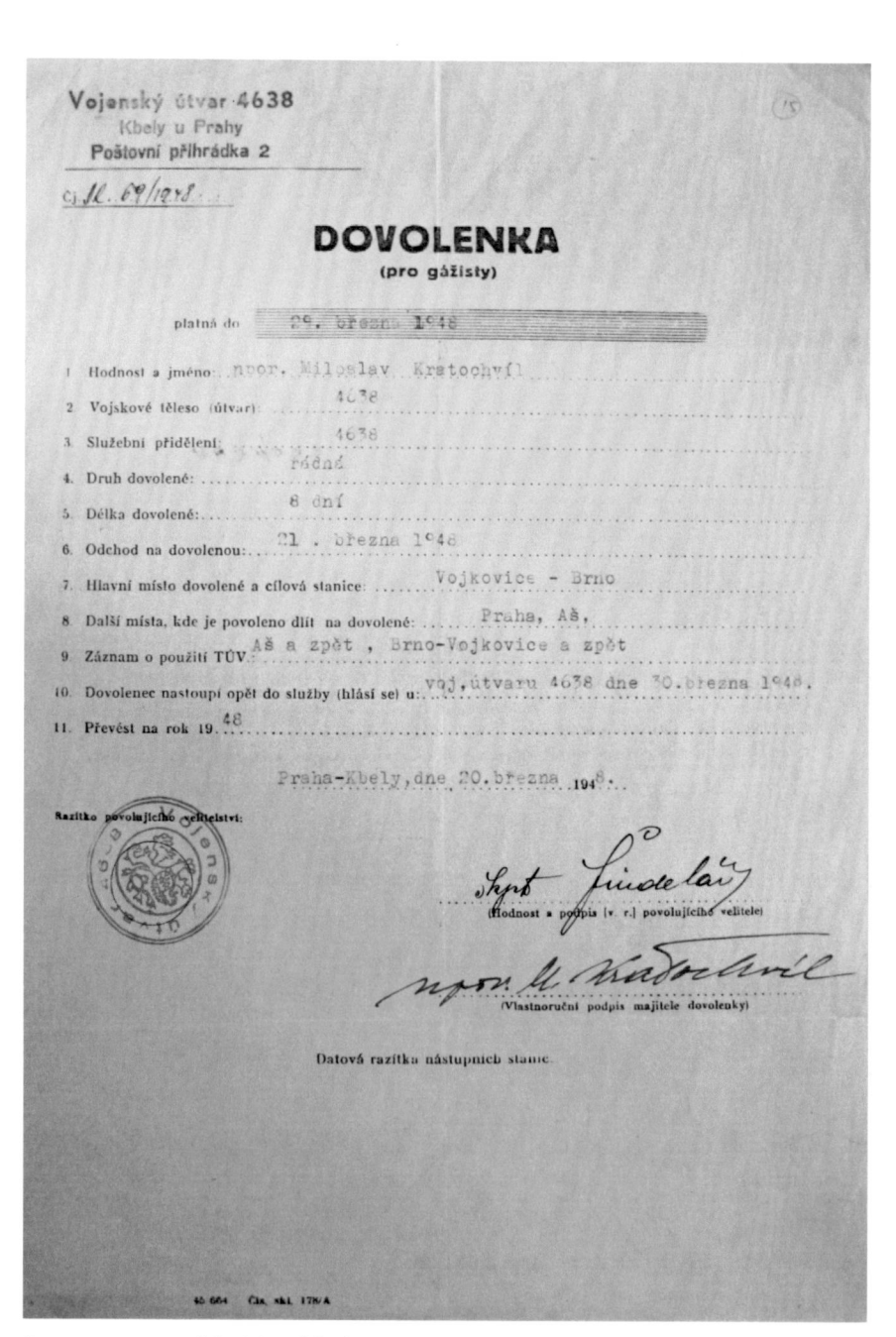

Leave pass, with Aš added as one of the destinations

My German health certificate - deloused with D.D.T.

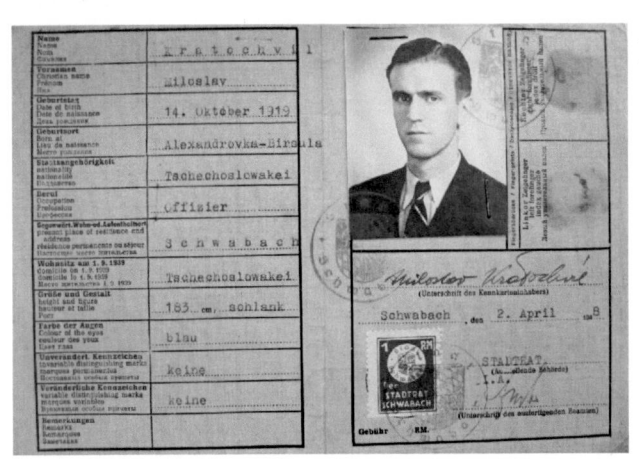

My German identity card "Kennkarte"

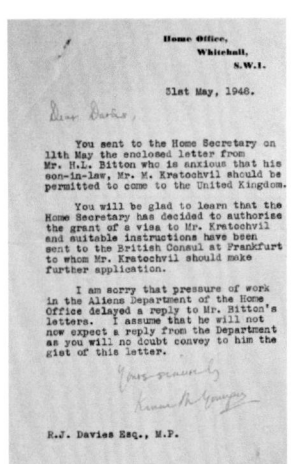

Home Office letter confirming my visa for entry to the UK

Chapter 9: England III

1948 June
After waiting in Wiesbaden for a few days, an American B52 Flying Fortress was able to take me to England, landing at Northolt on 10th June. The Immigration Officer stamped my temporary passport and let me through without even looking at any of my parcels. I had intended to show him the contents of what I was carrying. He simply refused to look at anything. (I was actually carrying some equipment, it could have been a typewriter, for Major Los, a Czech officer, because his flight to the UK had been delayed.) Now, at last, out of the terminal building, I felt really free! Everything was so peaceful. I did not have to look behind me any more. Even the policeman who had just stopped all the traffic on the main road to let a little boy cross was so friendly, so humane – and didn't even carry a gun!

    The train from Euston station brought me to Manchester where Joan and Tony were waiting to welcome me. It certainly was a lovely reunion. Joan's parents made me feel at home. Now every room in their house was occupied, as Lída Matys was still there. Joan and I had such a lot to tell each other. Joan's departure from Prague had been quite an adventure; she had been granted, and paid for, a travel permit on 25th March but for some reason this was no longer valid. A new permit, for another 20 Czech crowns, was granted on 30th March. She was able to leave Prague Airport, together with Joyce Foit, on Thursday 1st April. Before leaving, Joan had tidied the flat and placed my uniform and military gear on the kitchen table, so that there could be no accusations of my stealing government property! On 11th June, I went to report to the Manchester City Police, as specified on my visa permit (initially, I had to report every three months).

    Lída was still attending school and I tried to explain to her why her parents wanted her to remain in England. However, she would not hear of it. We wrote to and phoned her parents telling them about the situation. When Lída was able to speak to her parents on the phone she broke down, demanding to be allowed to go home. In July, Reverend V. Svoboda from Bratislava, who was a friend of the family and a member of the Czech Brethren, unexpectedly arrived to talk to her, trying to explain her parents' intentions. Even he failed to convince her about the seriousness of the situation. The 14-year old would not listen and at the end of term she went back home to

Bratislava. The following year, Jan Matys and his family were able to escape via Austria and reach the U.S.A.

Soon after my arrival, I started looking for employment. My first idea was to visit the Red Lion Brewery in Manchester, where a Czechoslovak brewer had been working during the war. He had given temporary jobs to many Czech soldiers while they were on leave. Even my brother Jaroslav had worked there. He explained to me that his free hand to arrange jobs had been very much curtailed, because of the unions. And the only job available just then was loading lorries with barrels of beer and it was not something he could recommend (the wages were £4 per week). He gave me the option of getting in touch with him again after a week. Joan's father was also trying to find some sort of employment for me. He arranged for me to meet a member of the Society of Friends (Quakers) for some advice on this matter. This was not much help either. Finding any job at all seemed rather hopeless. I decided to write to the Air Ministry regarding the possibility of re-joining the R.A.F. The answer came within a few days and I was asked to report to R.A.F. Cardington for an interview and medical. Eventually, I declined the Air Ministry offer which could easily have meant being posted abroad, due to domestic circumstances.

July – December
In the meantime, however, Joan's cousin, Kenneth Bitton, who lived on Grangethorpe Drive, had mentioned my situation to his work colleagues. Kenneth was in charge of a fleet of delivery vans at Birkett and Bostock, a bakery and confectionary company. One of the directors, Leon Birkett, had heard about my escape and the problems I was having trying to find employment. He sent a message, telling me to come and see him. During the war he had been a flying instructor and, after having a long chat with me, offered me a job in their subsidiary company, Robinson's (Caterers) Ltd, whose headquarters were in the centre of Manchester. I was simply delighted to be able to work and contribute towards the upkeep of my family. Everyone at home was pleased too! Mr. F. Robinson, one of the directors, introduced me to their buyer, Dr. Josef Einleger, and I was given a job in his department. My wages were £4.10s.0d. a week and being employed I also had to register at the National Insurance and Employment Office on Oldham Road, Manchester.

The company had eighteen branches, which included restaurants, cafés and snack bars as well as bread and cake shops, and employed about a hundred and eighty people, mostly female, except for the chefs and one or two of the managers. The buyer's department was responsible for supplying just about all the commodities, except bread and confectionary, sold or used at these outlets. Other exceptions were fresh meat and fish for the restaurants. Dr. Einleger's sister, Paula, also worked in the buyer's department. They were Austrian Jews who had been allowed to come to England in 1939 after the *Anschluss* of Austria by the Germans in 1938. During the war they had been interned on the Isle of Man. He had a doctorate in technology and spoke good English. He had already worked for the company for more than two years. His knowledge and guidance, especially at the beginning, was very much appreciated and helped me to understand the requirements of the business and to adjust to my new employment.

In July, I joined the Manchester South 690 Branch of the R.A.F. Association. The meetings were held at the Lloyd Hotel in Charlton-cum-Hardy. The branch had over 450 members, all of whom had been discharged from the services and the bulk of whom were now unemployed. I then realised how very lucky I had been, having been able to find employment so soon.

I wrote a letter to Air Mail, the official journal of the Association expressing my gratitude for the help given to me by Flt.Lt. R. Girdler, who was chairman of the R.A.F. Association branch in Frankfurt.

I got used to working in the buyer's department, though it was quite different from my previous military duties and flying. My pre-war apprenticeships and experience of working in delicatessens suddenly became useful. Joan also managed to find part-time work and this helped enormously towards our upkeep. Joan's parents were very kind and helpful while we strived to adjust to our new situation. After a few months with the company, I was sent to help out at various branches by Miss Vickers, who was the shops' supervisor. Some of the branches opened at 7.0 a.m. to serve early customers with cups of tea, coffee, sandwiches and cakes. At this time there was strict rationing: in homes, each person in a family was allocated a prescribed amount by the Ministry of Food. In shops, careful records of sales had to be kept, i.e. how many sandwiches, refreshments, meals, cigarettes, cups of tea and coffee, etc. had been sold and how many coupons for sweets had been used. These were then submitted monthly to the authorities as a basis for further allocations of foodstuffs, especially fats.

I managed to get home by 6.0 p.m. during the week and by 1.30 p.m. on Saturdays. This gave me enough spare time to pursue some sort of hobby and I was soon involved in rug making, producing rugs of all shapes and sizes for our own use, to sell and to give away as presents.

As we were starting our family life from scratch, I wrote to the Czechoslovak Relief Committee in London, enquiring whether we were eligible for financial aid. I had found out that a fund had been set up to assist escapees who needed help. Eventually, I was able to borrow £15 from them, which I repaid in monthly instalments of 10/-. Not long after Lída left to go home to Bratislava, Joan's parents and I were asked whether we could help a young Czechoslovak student to find a job in Manchester. His name was Ben Storek and he was sixteen or seventeen years old. He had been advised by his parents in Czechoslovakia not to return, and Reverend Svoboda had given him our address. With our help, he found a job with the New Day Furniture Company and was able to get accommodation at the YMCA. Some months later he got a better paid job at Quiligotti and Co. Ltd in Manchester. The following year, with the help of the Czechoslovak Relief Committee, he went to the U.S.A. to study at Harvard University. He married in the U.S.A. and visited us in 1975.

Joan quickly re-established contact with her childhood friends from the Garden Village. These included Nancy and Philip Gee, Barbara and Walter Williamson, her cousin Dorothy and Peter Dighton, and many others. They made us both very welcome. We felt rather awkward when we had to announce to Joan's parents that Joan was expecting another baby. We could see that this was bound to create problems, not only for them but also for us. And they became much more noticeable when Joan had to stay at home with her mother. On the other hand, I had always enjoyed a most cordial relationship with both her parents.

Jaroslav wrote to me from Germany, telling me about his second escape from Czechoslovakia on 12th October. The following year he managed to get a permit, with the help of our cousin Josef Kratochvíl in Saskatchewan, and on 16th March 1949 he arrived in Canada. While in the German DP camp he had met Josef Machek, who later went to U.S.A. He had also met Karol Vaculík in the DP camp, who had also helped escapees in 1939/40 when I brought them by train from Bratislava. Karol lived in Miloslavov, a village right on the Hungarian border. Jaroslav and Karol Vaculík eventually worked together on a building site in the Windsor area of Ontario. Jaroslav died there on 20th September 1950 in a railway accident.

My work at the different shops progressed well and I got used to serving customers and preparing sandwiches. I was keen to introduce the continental type of open sandwiches and Mrs. Robinson thought that it would be a good idea and brighten up our shop window by prominently displaying them. I started displaying them in one of the shops, with an assortment of over 24 different types. I later extended the idea to another two or three branches. The sandwiches were certainly admired very much, though actual sales were slow. Toppings included salami, gherkins, stuffed olives and anchovies – exotic ingredients to the general public, and they were seldom even willing to taste them! However, they did create an interesting talking point and, as intended, helped the window display.

1949 January – October
At home, everything was fine and the big day arrived on 24th April when John Leonard, his second name coming from Joan's father, was born. We were all delighted with the news. Joan and the baby were doing well and after about 14 days they came home from the nursing home. Although it became quite hectic in the house, Joan's parents were delighted at having another grandchild. It must have been very hard for them at their age to cope with all the extra problems that we had gradually imposed on them. We yearned to live somewhere else, on our own, but no opportunities were forthcoming. And with being away the whole day at work, I did not really grasp how strained the situation could become. Unfortunately, at this time the waiting list to acquire a house in the Garden Village had been closed. (The committee later allowed persons born in the Garden Village to put their names down on the waiting list and in this way we were able to register, finally moving there in 1953.)

During the summer, in my spare time – evenings and weekends – I joined the locals on the bowling green. The game was completely new to me and Joan's father was able to teach me some of the finer points, greatly increasing my enjoyment.

At work, I became more and more involved at the various branches, especially those requiring immediate help, whether due to the manageress being ill or poor performance in turnover and profit. All branches had to take weekly stocks of goods on Saturdays. The results of these were known by the following week on Wednesday or Thursday. Had any serious discrepancies occurred, I was asked to investigate and report the reasons to Mr. Robinson. I had to be very careful and tactful in my investigations. To many of the managers, I was a foreigner – an intruder – who might be after their jobs and many of the manageresses had been with the firm for a long time. The shop assistants were also all female. However, no formal qualifications were required to become one. It all seemed so very much different from Czechoslovakia. Later in the year, an opportunity arose for me to manage my own branch, at the Three Shires Restaurant in Spring Gardens. Parts of the premises had just been altered and a new entrance had been made from Fountain Street. It proved to be a very successful and profitable venture. I was able to show that I could manage the business to everyone's satisfaction, which also brought me an increase in wages to £5 per week. After a few months, I was appointed manager of a newly opened snack bar at 11 High Street, situated on the first floor above the shop. In fact, the whole building had been rented and the two floors above the snack bar were made into the head offices of Robinson's (Caterers) Ltd. Again, I was able to manage and establish this snack bar with great success, and created a good name for myself by introducing a few new dishes on the menu.

All the other branches, mostly selling bread, cakes, sandwiches and beverages, seemed to have rather low profit margins on their turnover. The figures at 'my' two snack bars indicated that something could be done and I suggested that some of the other branches could either be turned into snack bars or, if possible, a snack bar could be combined with their existing business. Of course, to put this idea into practice was a long-term plan and only tentatively discussed at my occasional meetings with Mr. Robinson. In the meantime, I was required to help Miss Vickers sort out existing problems at some of the other branches that were not performing too well. Also, after having successfully trained one of the staff at the High Street snack bar, I was able to hand it over to her to manage. Her name was Mrs. Price. I was very proud of her and she became a very good manageress.

In order to keep in touch with fellow servicemen and developments at 'home' in Czechoslovakia, I became a member of the Czechoslovak Legionaries-in-Exile and later also a member of the Free Czechoslovak Air Force Association in London.

On 14th October 1949, I celebrated my 30th birthday.

September, 1948   AIR MAIL

AN ALLY RETURNS

We have received the following very gratifying tribute from a Czechoslovak member whose name is withheld for obvious reasons :

"In March I crossed the Czechoslovak border on the run and found myself in a Refugee Camp in Germany. Conditions were pretty grim and one day in Frankfurt I saw a notice in a newspaper that the RAFA were forming a branch in Frankfurt. As an ex-RAF F/Sgt. I made inquiries, and contacted F/Lt. W. Girdler, who was one of the prime movers in forming the branch. From my first meeting with him many of my troubles were solved and I am writing to say how much I appreciate the ready help and kindly manner in which it was given. I am now with my wife, who is English, and we both wish to record how much we owe to the RAF Association."

AUSTRALIA CALLING

". . . it has occurred to us that this division might be able to help you in regard to Liaison Officers as far as Australia is concerned. We have already been

My letter to Air Mail, the Official Journal of the RAFA, September 1948

Decision of the Supreme Military Court to confiscate our flat in Prague

177

Postscript

What happened next? 1949 was a long time ago and it would take another book to recount events to the present date. However, I would like to record the following:

In January 1951 my father was naturalised, which meant that he no longer had to report to the Manchester City Police. As there were often difficulties with regard to the spelling and pronunciation of Kratochvíl, it was decided in 1953 to change our family name to Bitton, my mother's maiden name.

Both before and after retirement he was actively involved in the local R.A.F. Association and the Association of Czechoslovak Legionaries Abroad, taking part in numerous supportive activities and commemorative events.

Due to the post-war political climate in Czechoslovakia, it was not possible for him to visit his homeland and it was not until 1966 that his mother was allowed to visit us. Circumstances changed rapidly after the Velvet Revolution at the end of 1989, and in the summer of 1991 he was at last able to visit his family and friends again for the first time in 43 years. A couple of months later he participated in a rehabilitation ceremony for former R.A.F. airmen in Prague, gaining public recognition for his services to the Czechoslovak state during the war. My mother and I were also present and it was a most moving occasion: the official acknowledgement, the reception held by President Havel in Prague Castle and the spontaneous appreciation offered by complete strangers.

In 2010 he took part in the 70th anniversary ceremony at Cholmondeley Castle to commemorate the establishment of the Czechoslovak Army in England in 1940. On this occasion he was acknowledged for his 'life-long work in favour of the Czechoslovak Legionary Community, for extraordinary merits in defence of the Republic and for upholding general awareness of Czechoslovak soldiers in the United Kingdom'.

My father celebrated his 94th birthday in October. He now lives in a retirement home in Mobberley, near Knutsford.

Finally, I would like to take this opportunity to give special thanks to Lotta Fischerström for typing the major part of the manuscript and to John Kolbert, the Secretary of the Association of Czechoslovak Legionaries Abroad, for his help in editing and producing this book.

I would also like to apologize for any inconsistences or inaccuracies – the contents of the book are to a large extent based on personal notes and memories of events that took place a time long ago.

John Bitton
November 2013
Helsingborg, Sweden

Military Service

Czechoslovak Infantry Battalion No. 11 – East
November 1940 to   Civilian volunteer, Lance Corporal
May 1942

200th Czechoslovak Light Anti-Aircraft Regiment – East
May 1942 to   Lance Corporal
1 January 1943

Royal Air Force
2 January 1943	AC2
7 May 1943	LAC
24 March 1944	Sergeant, R.A.F. wings awarded
4 January 1945	Posted to 310 Squadron, serving at R.A.F. Stations North Weald, Bradwell Bay and Manston
24 March to 21 September 1945	Flight Sergeant, 310 Squadron at R.A.F. Manston

Czechoslovak Air Force
22 September 1945	Continued service in Czechoslovak Air Force as Flight Sergeant (310 Squadron was formally disbanded on 15 February 1946)
4 March 1946	Commissioned, backdated to 1 January
1 January 1946	*Podporučík*, Second Lieutenant (Pilot Officer)
1 July 1946	*Nadporučík*, First Lieutenant (Flying Officer)

Honorary promotion after rehabilitation of former R.A.F. pilots in 1991
13 September 1991	*Podplukovník*, Lieutenant Colonel (Wing Commander)
8 May 1995	*Plukovník*, Colonel (Group Captain)

Decorations, Czechoslovakia

7 March 1944	*Pamětní medaile československé armády v zahraničí 1943* Commemorative Medal of the Czechoslovak Army Abroad 1943
15 March 1945	*Československá vojenská medaile Za zásluhy 1943 I. stupně* Czechoslovak Military Medal for Merit, 1943, Grade I
18 August 1945	*Československá medaile Za chrabrost před nepřítelem 1940* Czechoslovak Medal for Gallantry in the Face of the Enemy 1940
2 March 1946	*Československý válečný kříž 1939-1945* Czechoslovak War Cross 1939-1945 Service in the Middle East and R.A.F.
30 November 1946	*Štefánikův pamětní odznak II. stupně* Stefanik Commemorative Badge, Grade II
26 February 1947	*Československý válečný kříž 1939-1945* Czechoslovak War Cross 1939-1945 Participation in the national struggle for liberation
26 February 1947	*Československá vojenská medaile Za zásluhy 1943 I. stupně* Czechoslovak Military Medal for Merit, 1943, Grade I Underground activities, establishing and running escape routes

Decorations, United Kingdom

1945	1939-1945 Star
1945	Africa Star. Clasp, 8th Army
1945	France and Germany Star
1996[1]	Defence Medal
1996[1]	War Medal 1939-1945

Decorations, Poland

1991 — *Krzyż Czynu Bojowego Polskich Sił Zbrojnych na Zachodzie* Military Action Cross, Polish Armed Forces in the West with Tobruk Clasp

Decorations, Czech Republic

4 July 2010 — *Čestný odznak Armády České republiky Za zásluhy 1. stupně* Honorary badge of the Armed Forces of the Czech Republic for Merits, Grade I. For life-long work in favour of the Czechoslovak Legionary Community, for extraordinary merits in defence of the Republic and for upholding general awareness of Czechoslovak soldiers in the United Kingdom.

---

[1] Campaign medals for service 1939-1945 confirmed by the Ministry of Defence on 19 June 1996.

Commemorative medals, Czechoslovakia

Czechoslovak Legionaries medal

Commemorative medals, Czech Republic
2000   60th Anniversary medal, Czechoslovak Army Abroad

2005   60th Anniversary medal, end of WWII

Commemorative medals, Slovak Republic
1995   Victory medal, 50th Anniversary of end of WWII

1995   50th Anniversary of liberation of Slovakia and end of WWII

2005   60th Anniversary medal, end of WWII

Commemorative medals
2010   70th Anniversary merit badge, Czechoslovak Army in England

2010   70th Anniversary of Czechoslovak airmen joining the R.A.F. and 65th Anniversary of the Liberation of Czechoslovakia, Gold Medal, Governor of South Moravia

Badges
Czechoslovak Army badge and Czechoslovak Pilots' Association badge

Also Published by Melandrium Books:

My Struggle For Freedom
By Josef Novák
Price £10